100
Quick&Easy
Worship Ideas for Kids

Karen Holford

Pacific Press® Publishing Association
Nampa, Idaho
Oshawa, Ontario, Canada
www.pacificpress.com

Other books by Karen Holford

100 Creative Prayer Ideas for Kids
I Miss Grandpa
Danger at Deerwood Grove

Designed by Linda Griffith

Copyright © 2004 by
Pacific Press® Publishing Association
Printed in United States of America
All Rights Reserved

Additional copies of this book are available by calling toll free 1-800-765-6955 or visiting http://www.adventistbookcenter.com.

Library of Congress Cataloging-in-Publication Data

Holford, Karen.
100 quick and easy worship ideas for kids / Karen Holford.
p. cm.
ISBN: 0-8163-2051-9
1. Family—Religious life. 2. Children—Religious life. I. Title: One hundred quick and easy worship ideas for kids. II. Title.

BV4526.3.H64 2004
249—dc22   2003070701

04 05 06 07 08 • 5 4 3 2 1

Dedication

Especially for Heather, Lez, Daniel, and Michael,
and all the other young families we know.

To busy, tired, and overstretched parents everywhere,
who long to share God creatively with their families;
and to their lively, curious children,
whose hearts are filled with wonder, simplicity, and innocence.

May each of you find new ways to experience God
through the ideas in this book.

Acknowledgments

Thank you, Heather, for enthusiastically sharing your thoughts with me
when I was struggling with the last twenty ideas.

Thank you, Bernie, and our children, Bethany, Nathan, and Joel, for
cleaning the house, cooking, and going surfing,
while I stayed at home to write!

Thank you, Tim and the team at Pacific Press,
for encouraging me to write another book.
It was so much fun!

And thank You, God, for the inspiration of Your Holy Spirit,
without whom this project could never have been completed
in the tiny window of time in which I had to write.

Contents

A prayer for this book

Father God,
we praise You for all Your love and inspiration,
for Your creativity and greatness,
and for Your attention to the tiniest details of our lives.

We praise You for bodies that move, sense, grow, and learn.
We praise You for the wonderful world that still looks so beautiful,
even after all these years.
Thank You for seasons and changes and celebrations.
Thank You for the amazing stories of Your power and love
that still inspire and comfort us.
And thank You that You care about our happiness as a family,
and that You smile when we have fun together.

In all these ways we want to worship You
and to teach our children about You.
Open our eyes and our hearts with wonder.
May we become as little children and learn again about Your love for us.
May we find delight in sharing You with our beloved children.
And may we all grow closer to You as we discover You,
and worship You together.

May the grace of Jesus be experienced in our homes.
May the Holy Spirit inspire us.
And may the love of the Father be wrapped around us,
binding us together.
In Jesus' name,
Amen.

Introduction

How to help your child grow spiritually

The most important gift we can give our children is the desire to love God and to follow and serve Him.

- Parents can help their children by being a positive role model, because children are encouraged by their parents' faith.
- It's very important that you nurture your own spiritual development through Bible study, prayer, meditation, etc. This book contains thoughts for you, to help stimulate your own spiritual development.
- Talk to your child about your own faith and relationship with God in ways that she[1] can understand too.
- Pray for your family and your child, as well as for yourself. Let your child see and hear you praying for her. Share suitable stories of answered prayer with your child, to help her develop trust in God.
- Help your child to look for answers to prayer but also to understand that God knows best, and sometimes the answers come in ways that we're not expecting or even wanting.
- Experience God's grace and forgiveness for yourself so that you can pass this on to your child. Grace is about God loving us no matter what we have done, just because we are His children. This is one of the most beautiful aspects of the Christian faith.
- Learn how to put God's grace into action in your family, by offering forgiveness and showing acceptance when your child makes mistakes or accidentally breaks or spoils something.
- Deal with your child in the way God has patiently dealt with you. Think about how God has gently disciplined you before you consider how to discipline your child in a way that will bring her closer to God.
- As you parent your child, aim to show God's amazing love for her by the way you manage her with caring gentleness. Read 1 Corinthians 13 and

---

[1] Throughout this book, "he" and "she" will be used interchangeably in reference to your child. However, all the activities are suitable for both boys and girls.

think about how that kind of love can make a difference to your parenting.

- Create regular interesting worships to share with your child. This book will give you some ideas that you can adapt in different ways to provide a rich resource of worship activities.

Guidelines for great family worships

Here are some guidelines to help your family have special worships, and ideas to help you fill them with interesting activities for you and your child.

- As parents, make sure you are being filled spiritually through your own meaningful worship times.
- Keep the family worships simple. One idea is to use a devotional book suitable for the age of your child, with short inspirational stories, during the week.
- Make weekend worship times as special as you can.
- Plan ahead for worships, and gather the materials you need well before time.
- Invest in the best spiritual material for your child! Buy good books from your local Christian book store, seek out and rent good Christian videos, and buy interesting Bible games and activity books.
- Keep worship times free of discipline and criticism. Make them positive experiences that are fun, interesting, brief, happy, and loving. This is what your child will remember the most.
- Use the worships to learn Bible stories, learn how to make good choices, follow God's guidance, develop a prayer relationship with God, learn about God's creation, memorize scriptures, experience the joy of serving others in practical ways, learn worshipful songs, and enjoy being a Christian.
- Remember that children learn in different ways, and make sure that your worships contain practical illustrations, crafts, memorable stories, and physical activities.
- Use the everyday events that happen to you and your child to teach them about God. Opportunities for spiritual teaching are all around you once you start to look, and these are often the best ways to help your child learn about God. This book includes many worships that can be blended into the usual family routines with very little effort.

How to use this book

This book is full of different ideas that could enhance your family worships. It has been laid out to help you plan worships quickly. Following are some explanations of the different sections.

Bible stories:
- Some suggestions are included for Bible stories that may be connected with the worship activity. These suggestions are not exhaustive, and you may think of others that you could use. You might like to jot these other ideas in your book for future reference.

Things you need:
- It can be very helpful to create a worship box so that regularly needed items are close at hand. The following things may be useful to put in the box:

Child's Bible	Marker pens	Brass fasteners
Safe scissors	Pencils	Bubbles
Adhesive tape	Eraser	Magazine pictures
Stick adhesive	String	Bible story books
White paper	Balloons	Musical instruments
Colored paper	Crayons	A soft scarf for a blindfold
Colored card	Paper plates	Brown lunch sacks
A scrapbook	Stickers	Fabric scraps

Worship activities:
- Every child and every family is different, so not every activity will suit every child or family. It is up to you to choose the activities that best suit your family's needs.
- Preschool children vary widely in their abilities and interests. Activities that may not work now may be more suitable in a year's time.
- Many of these worships are designed to need very little preparation, because parents of preschoolers are usually very busy. You can even send your child to help you find some of the things you need for worship.
- You may want to have a simple worship on weekdays, and save some of the more complex or longer worships for the weekends.

Another option:
- Many of the worships also include other options that may suit you better, or in case you don't have everything you need for the first worship idea. These can also be developed to provide extra worships for you and your child.
- Many preschoolers like to repeat worships that they enjoy, so note the ones that your child would like to try again.

Just for you:
- Thoughts for you have also been included because parents often feel that their own spiritual life is neglected. By providing things for you to think about, you can experience your child's worship theme at a different spiritual level.

Bible verses:
- Bible verses are provided for your own meditation, but they may also be suitable as memory verses for your child.

Learning memory verses
Learning a memory verse can be a challenge for preschool children who don't yet read. Try some of these activities to help your child learn:
- Make up actions for the Bible verse that suit the words, and act the verse out as it is said. Let your child make up her own actions.
- Set the words of the verse to a well-known tune and make it into a song. Some Bible verses are already songs, and you could see how many of these songs your family could learn.
- Rebus puzzles replace some of the words with little pictures. Write out the verse using simple pictures instead of some of the words. Younger children who can't read can use the picture clues to help them learn the verse.
- Stand in a circle and throw a ball from one person to another across the middle of the circle, so no one quite knows who will catch the ball next. When the ball is caught, the catcher has to say the next word in the Bible verse, before throwing the ball to the next person. See how quickly you can go! For a bigger challenge, stand farther apart.
- Make the Bible verse into an attractive poster. Or illustrate some of the Proverbs with cartoons.

Music for worship
- Add music to your worship by using CDs or cassettes of children's worship songs.
- Buy some videos of children's Christian songs for your child to watch. She will soon learn the songs as she sings along.
- Make or buy a collection of simple musical instruments that your child can play during worship.
- Create your own praise songs by using tunes you already know and adding your own words. Ask your child for ideas.
- Add actions to all kinds of songs to help your active child enjoy the music.
- Choose lively songs especially written for small children.
- Be sure that the songs reflect your own beliefs, and that you enjoy the music too.

God Loves Me!

One of the most important things a child can learn about God is just how much God loves him. Children learn about God's love by experiencing the love of their parents. Parents pass on the love of God when they have experienced it for themselves.

Remember that God is forever loving you and trying to touch you with His love.

He delights in you.

He heals you.

He forgives you.

He remembers that you are fragile and that you get tired.

He cares about you and your family.

He knows that you are doing the most important job on earth as you share His love with your child, and He is there for you all the time. When things seem the darkest, He is the closest.

Read Psalm 103 and spend time thinking about God's amazing love, just for you, and then share that love with your child.

1

God loves me all the time

Bible stories:
David and Bathsheba—2 Samuel 11; 12
Zacchaeus—Luke 19:1-10

THINGS YOU NEED:

- paper plate
- brass fastener to secure the hands to the clock and let them rotate
- cardboard to make clock hands
- marker pen
- twelve heart stickers

Worship activities:

1. Make a simple clock out of the plate, adding hands that turn. Add numbers to the clock.

2. Write "God loves me all the time" on the clock.

3. Ask your child twelve questions. For example:

Does God love you when you are asleep? When you are playing? When you don't want to eat your vegetables? When you accidentally break something? When you disobey Mom or Dad? When you forget to pray? When you put your shoes on the wrong feet? When you are sick?

4. Every time your child says Yes, give him a heart sticker to put next to a number on the clock.

Another option:

- Purchase a flashing heart pin for your child to wear for a day. The pin will flash no matter how he behaves, as a reminder that God loves the child even when he is not perfect.

Just for you:

- Why not use a flashing heart pin to remind you that God loves you all the time, too, even when you get tired and frustrated?

" 'I have loved you with an everlasting love; I have drawn you with loving-kindness' " (Jeremiah 31:3).

When you are happy? When you are sad?
When you push your brother?
When you pick a pretty flower for your Mom?

13

2

God loves me and wants to forgive me

Bible stories:
David and Bathsheba—2 Samuel 11; 12
Zacchaeus—Luke 19:1-10
Jesus heals the paralytic man—Matthew 9:1-8

THINGS YOU NEED:

• pot of bubbles

Worship activities:

1. Tell your child that God loves us very much and wants to forgive us when we have done things wrong.

2. Take the pot of bubbles and say, "Please God, forgive me for . . ." and name something you have said or done wrong. Then blow the bubbles.

3. Tell your child that just as the bubbles pop and completely disappear, so God takes our sins away when we tell Him about them. It's important not to pop the bubbles, because the idea is that God does everything for us—it's not something we can do for ourselves.

4. Then let your child confess a sin, blow the bubbles, and watch as they float away and burst.

5. Tell your child that God forgives us because He looks at Jesus and not us.

6. Jesus has done all the work so that we don't have to.

7. Thank God for Jesus and His forgiveness!

Just for you:

• Take the time to experience God's forgiveness. It is much easier to forgive others when we feel forgiven ourselves.

• Blowing bubbles is great for distressed grown-ups too!

"If we confess our sins, he is faithful and just and will forgive us our sins and purify us from all unrighteousness" (1 John 1:9).

3

God provides for all of our needs

Bible stories:
Manna in the wilderness—Exodus 16
Elijah and the ravens—1 Kings 17:1-6
Elijah and the widow of Zarephath—1 Kings 17:7-16
Jesus feeds the five thousand—Matthew 14:13-21

T H I N G S   Y O U   N E E D :
- an attractive basket

Worship activities:
1. Talk to your child about how God provides for our needs.
2. Together, think about the things you really need that God has provided for you, such as clothes, food, money, water, warmth, and a car.
3. Send your child on a scavenger hunt to find a piece of clothing, a toy car, a can of food, a cup, a scarf, a coin, and other such items.
4. Place all the things in the basket and thank God for what He has provided.
5. Let your child take the things back to their places.

Another option:
- Talk about how God gives us extra things to share with others who have a greater need. Let your child help you pack a bag of groceries for a local charity and come with you to deliver them.

Just for you:
- Do you have a need as a parent? Tell God about it, and then find a way to invite another adult to help meet that need for you.
- Do you have a friend who has a need too? Perhaps you could help meet each other's needs for support, friendship, child care, and so on.

"My God will meet all your needs according to his glorious riches in Christ Jesus" (Philippians 4:19).

4

God loves me and never forgets me

Bible story:
Joseph—Genesis 37; 39–47

THINGS YOU NEED:
- tray with about ten familiar but very different items on it (cup, hairbrush, teddy bear, fork, book, shoe, sock, can of beans, apple, flower)
- towel to hide the tray full of objects

Worship activities:
1. Play the memory game:
   a. Show your child the tray of ten objects.
   b. Let your child touch the objects and look at them for a few minutes.
   c. Cover up the tray.
   d. See how many things your child can remember. Prompt him a little but try to let him forget at least one thing!
   e. As the child remembers items, bring the items out from under the towel.
2. Talk about how God never forgets us. We are always in His mind because He loves us.
3. Thank Him for remembering us all the time, even when we are hidden away or when we feel other people have forgotten us.

Another option:
- If your child has a simple memory card game, play that instead of the tray game.

Just for you:
- What did God do for you today to let you know that He hasn't forgotten you? Perhaps you could keep a diary and write one thing each day that God has done to show you that He always remembers you.
- Has someone you know forgotten how much God loves them? How can you show them God's love and encourage them?

"I will not forget you" (Isaiah 49:15).

5

God loves me and wants me to be with Him

Bible stories:
Heaven—John 14:1-3
The New Jerusalem—Revelation 21; 22

THINGS YOU NEED:

• two towels

Worship activities:

1. Place a towel at each end of the room. Call one towel "heaven" and one towel "earth."

2. Tell your child that God loves him very much and wants us all to be together one day. Have your child stand on the "earth" towel while you stand on the "heaven" towel, and ask him to jump to you without touching the floor or any of the furniture.

3. Allow time for your child to realize that this is impossible to do.

4. Say that you can help the child get to the "heaven" towel if he would like to come and join you.

5. When the child decides to come, walk over, pick him up in your arms, and carry him back to the "heaven" towel.

6. Explain that Jesus is coming to take us to heaven so that He can show us how much He loves us forever.

Another option:

• If you have stairs, you could stand at the top and ask your child to come up the stairs to you, without touching the walls, the railing, or the steps. When he realizes that this is impossible, come down the stairs to meet your child and carry him up the stairs. Do this only if it is safe.

Just for you:

• What do you most look forward to in heaven? Talk about this with a friend.

"'And if I go and prepare a place for you, I will come back and take you to be with me' " (John 14:3).

6

God loves me and wants me to be happy

Bible stories:
Ruth and Naomi—book of Ruth
Hannah and Samuel—I Samuel 1:1–2:11
Esther—book of Esther

THINGS YOU NEED:
- three sheets of white printer paper folded to make a book
- needle and thread to stitch the book together through the fold
- pictures from magazines
- crayons, adhesive, scissors
- smiley-face stickers

Worship activities:
1. Make a small booklet for your child by folding the paper in half and stitching through the fold.
2. Talk to the child about the things that make him really happy.
3. Write the child's answers in the book and then draw or paste pictures in the book to illustrate the answers.
4. Let your child stick a smiley-face sticker on every page.
5. Tell your child that God loves him so much that He wants him to be as happy as possible.

Other options:
- Take photos of the things that make your child happy and put them in the book.
- Instead of a booklet, make a poster of happy things.
- Make a booklet of the happy stories that happen to your child.

Just for you:
- What makes you happy? Look out for happy moments and fun stories to share at family mealtimes.
- Do you know what brings happiness to the other members of your family? If you discover what makes them happy, you may be able to serve God by adding to their happiness.

"Rejoice in the Lord always. I will say it again: Rejoice!" (Philippians 4:4).

7

God sends His angels to help look after me

Bible stories:
Daniel in the lions' den—Daniel 6
Jesus in the wilderness—Matthew 4:1-11
Peter in prison—Acts 12:1-19

THINGS YOU NEED:
- objects that could remind your child of other people who help take care of them in different ways, such as:
  - toothbrush—dentist
  - medicine—doctor
  - cookie cutter—Grandma
  - tractor—Grandpa
  - lunchbox—day-care or preschool teacher

Worship activities:
1. Ask your child who helps take care of them.
2. Show the objects and see if they remind your child of any caring people.
3. Explain that although you do everything you can to take care of your child, you need other people to help you from time to time, so that you can care for him in the very best way.
4. God loves us very much, and He knows about us all the time, but He still has angels that help take care of us in the very best way possible.
5. Thank God for your child's guardian angel.

Other options:
- Tell the story of a time when a guardian angel protected you or your child.
- Use simple objects to create a small angel to hang in your child's room or in your car. Use the angel as a reminder to thank God for sending angels to care for you and your child.

Just for you:
- If you wrote a Thank-you letter to your guardian angel, what would you be most thankful for?

"For he will command his angels concerning you to guard you in all your ways" (Psalm 91:11).

8

God knows everything about me

Bible story:
Psalm 139

THINGS YOU NEED:

- paper and pencil

Worship activities:

1. Ask your child to draw a picture of himself.
2. Ask your child how well the child thinks he knows himself.
3. Ask your child the following questions:
   a. How many toes do you have?
   b. How many legs?
   c. How many fingers?
   d. How many eyes?
   e. How many ears?
   f. How many teeth?
   g. How many hairs?
4. Each time your child answers a question, write the number next to that body part on his portrait. If counting is still hard for your child, help him count with you.
5. Even though your child knows himself really well, there are still things he can never know, such as how many hairs are on his head. Even counting our own teeth can be hard!
6. But God knows everything, all the time. Even though He doesn't really need to know how many hairs are on our heads, He still knows, because He cares about us so much.
7. Thank God in your prayers for all your fingers and toes and ears and eyes and teeth and hairs.

Other options:

- Make fingerprints with your child, using a washable, nontoxic inkpad.
- Show your child how each fingerprint is different. Show how your fingerprints are different from his. Perhaps you could collect the index fingerprints of every family member and see if you can guess which belongs to each one.

8

Just for you:

- In what ways has God made you unique? What do you appreciate about the unique ways He has made you? What do you appreciate about the uniqueness of your other family members?

"You are familiar with all my ways" (Psalm 139:3).

9

God knows my name

Bible stories:
The boy Samuel—1 Samuel 3
The calling of Abram—Genesis 15

THINGS YOU NEED:
- book of names and their meanings
- paper, pencils, crayons, stick adhesive
- variety of pictures from magazines or from computer clip art

Worship activities:
1. Talk to your child about his name. Tell him why you chose the name you did, and how you chose that name from thousands of others.

2. Tell your child that you are going to play a game. He must go just outside the room and come in when he is called.

3. Call out three different names and then call the child's name. Do this several times.

4. Then take the paper and make a picture of your child's name. Draw the outlines of the letters and let your child color the letters. Write the meaning of your child's name on the paper, and then cut out some pictures to illustrate the meaning. Paste these pictures around your child's name.

5. Tell your child that God knows him by name. He doesn't ever forget or get our names muddled up, as other people might do. He knows our names because He loves us very much and we are important to Him.

6. Create a special prayer of blessing for your child, using the letters of his name to help you form an acrostic prayer, in which each phrase begins with a letter of his name. For example:

Dear Father, thank You for Sam. Please bless him.
S—Send your angels to watch over him.
A—Always keep him safe.
M—May he choose to do what is right.
In Jesus' name, Amen.

Another option:
- Use a computer graphics program to create a name picture by using interesting word art. Add the meaning of your child's name and any pictures that illustrate the meaning. Then print out the page and frame it to go in his room.

22

Just for you:

• What does your name mean? Why were you given your name? What do you like about your name? Who are the people who call your name and you feel delighted? Who are the people who call your name and your heart sinks?

• Imagine God calling your name in the most loving way He could. How would you respond to His call?

> *" 'I have summoned you by name; you are mine' "*
> *(Isaiah 43:1).*

10

God provides for our clothes

Bible stories:
Joseph's coat—Genesis 37:3
Hannah makes a coat for Samuel—1 Samuel 2:18-21
Dorcas makes clothes for the children—Acts 9:36-43

THINGS YOU NEED:
- basket
- pile of clothes for different occasions

Worship activities:
1. Place a pile of clothes in a basket. Choose clothes that cover a range of occasions, such as swimsuits, scarves, church clothes, rain gear, hats, shorts, and sunglasses.
2. Ask your child to find the clothes he would wear at different times. If the child chooses something that doesn't seem appropriate to you, ask him if he would like to wear something else as well, or ask him questions about when he would usually wear that piece of clothing.
3. Pray by letting your child choose his favorite clothes and put them on in whatever arrangement the child likes. Then let him thank God for the clothes, or for each individual item he is wearing.
4. Pray for those who don't have enough clothes.

Other options:
- Use paper dolls for this activity instead of real clothes.
- Show your child how to fold all the clothes you have used, so that they are neat and ready to go back in his closet. Talk about the importance of taking good care of the clothes God provides for us.
- Make a scrapbook page of pictures of clothes from catalogs, and write "Thank You, God, for my clothes."
- Help your child to choose some outgrown clothes to take to a charity.

Just for you:
- Sort through your clothes and choose some to pass on to a charitable organization. Or purchase some gift vouchers for your favorite clothing store and give them secretly to a person you know who may not be able to afford many

10

new clothes. As you give, thank God for providing your clothes, and enjoy being part of God's plan to provide for other people's clothing needs.

" 'Therefore I tell you, do not worry . . . about your body,
what you will wear' " (Matthew 6:25).

God provides good things for us to eat

Bible stories:
Manna in the wilderness—Exodus 16
Elijah and the ravens—1 Kings 17:1-6
Feeding the five thousand—Matthew 14:13-21

THINGS YOU NEED:
- selection of attractive fruit cut into manageable pieces
- bamboo skewers and plates
- sweet sauce, syrup, or dip in a bowl

Worship activities:
1. Talk about the different fruits, their flavors, textures, and colors, and how God created them for us to enjoy.
2. Invite your child to choose her favorite fruits and thread them onto the bamboo skewer. Take care that no one gets poked by the skewers.
3. Cover the fruit skewers with plastic wrap and save them for dessert, or eat them right away. Dip the fruit in the sauce if you like.
4. Thank God for all the many different fruits He has created for us to eat.

Other options:
- Make a fruit salad together. Even small children can cut bananas with a blunt knife. Or arrange slices of fruit to make a face on a plate.
- Make banana popsicles by sliding a popsicle stick into the banana, coating the banana with honey, peanut butter, or chocolate/carob spread, and rolling the coated banana in coconut, finely chopped nuts, grated chocolate, or some other topping. Freeze for a few hours to make healthy ice cream.

Just for you:
- Read Galatians 5:22, 23 and think about the fruit of the Spirit. Which fruits could remind you of the different spiritual fruits?
- Which fruits are in your spiritual fruit salad? Are there some other fruits you would like to see in your salad? How could you work with the Holy Spirit to cultivate these fruits?

"But the fruit of the Spirit is love, joy, peace, patience, kindness, good-ness, faithfulness, gentleness and self-control" (Galatians 5:22, 23).

12

God provides us with good water to drink

Bible stories:
> The water that came from the rock—Exodus 17:1-7
> Hagar and Ishmael in the desert—Genesis 21:8-19
> The woman at the well—John 4:1-38

THINGS YOU NEED:

- good drinking water
- two glasses
- dirt

Worship activities:

1. Fill two glasses with water, one clean and one with dirt in it. Stir the dirt around so that the water is obviously dirty.

2. Offer your child a drink of water, showing the two glasses.

3. Give your child the clean water.

4. Say, "When we're thirsty it's nice to drink fresh, clear water."

5. But not everyone has such nice clear water. Sometimes the only water to drink is dirty and smelly. Show your child the other glass. Would she like to drink that water?

6. Thank God that you have plenty of lovely clear water to drink, and pray for the people who don't have good water to drink.

Another option:

- Perhaps you and your child could find out how much money is needed to dig a well for a family or village. Could you work together with friends to raise the money for a well somewhere?

Just for you:

- What could you do to stay in touch with God all through your day? Perhaps you could buy a promise box and keep it near your sink or desk. Each time you drink a glass of water, read another text and meditate on it.

" 'Whoever drinks the water I give him will never thirst' "
(John 4:14).

13

God gives us our homes

Bible stories:
Abram and Sarah traveling from place to place—Genesis 12; 13
The Shunammite woman building a room for Elisha—2 Kings 4:8-37
Mary, Martha, and Lazarus—Luke 10:38-42

T H I N G S   Y O U   N E E D :

- large cardboard box from a kitchen appliance store
- scissors
- thick black marker pen

Worship activities:
1. Talk to your child about your home. Perhaps you built it yourself. Tell your child the story of how God provided your home for you.
2. Take the big box and work together with your child to make a playhouse out of the box by carefully cutting windows and a door in the sides.
3. Have fun with the house for a while and then think about what it would be like to live in a cardboard box. What would happen when it rains or snows? Is there enough space inside for everything you need? How long would the house last?
4. Thank God for your house. Walk through your home together, thanking God for all the different rooms you have. Walk outside and feel the walls and thank Him for good, thick walls and a roof to keep you warm and dry and safe.

Another option:
- Use a small cardboard milk carton, shaped like a house. Wash it well and then cover it with peanut butter. Decorate it with breadsticks and crackers to make a small edible house.

Just for you:
- Walk through your home and let your prayers be inspired by your rooms.
- In the hallway, invite God into your home; in the kitchen, thank Him for providing for you; and so on. Or find other inspiration from the themes of your rooms.

"Unless the Lord builds the house, its builders labor in vain"
(Psalm 127:1).

God gives us our families

Bible stories:
Abraham, Sarah, and baby Isaac—Genesis 21:1-8
Isaac and Rebekah and their twins—Genesis 25:20-26
Mary, Joseph, and Jesus—Luke 2

THINGS YOU NEED:
• photos of family members

Worship activities:
1. Hug your child and tell her how much you love her, and how she is a special gift given to you by God.
2. Talk about the other members of your family and how they are all special gifts from God. How are the people different? How are they the same? What is good about having a family?
3. As you look at the photographs of the different family members, talk about the happy memories you have of each of them.
4. Use the photos in your prayer and pray for each person as you look at their picture.

Another option:
• Use a simple photo album and insert photos and prayer requests so that each person's prayer needs are on the page facing their photograph.

Just for you:
• What do you appreciate about some of your different family members? Have you ever told them? Perhaps you could find a way to share your appreciation with them.

"Better a meal of vegetables where there is love than a fattened calf with hatred" (Proverbs 15:17).

15

God provides toys for me to play with

Bible stories:
Jesus and the children—Luke 18:16, 17

THINGS YOU NEED:
• selection of your child's favorite toys

Worship activities:
1. Show your child a few of her favorite toys.
2. Ask your child to choose a favorite toy from the pile. Ask why this toy is so special and what she enjoys about the toy.
3. Then ask the child to choose the favorite toy from those that are left, and repeat the questions.
4. Do this again for the third favorite toy.
5. Explain that God is happy when the child is happy. God provides the money for all the things that we have, so God has provided for toys as well.
6. Thank God for the toys, and invite your child to give thanks for each toy by saying, "Thank You, God, for my _____. I like it very much because _____. Amen."

Other options:
• Take your child to buy a toy similar to her favorite toy to give to a charity that provides Christmas gifts for needy children.
• Find some stickers with the smiling face of Jesus on them. Stick these on your child's favorite toys.

Just for you:
• What do you like to do for fun? Do something fun today for a few moments, and thank God for the enjoyment it brings to you. Perhaps you could share your fun activity with someone else and invite them to play for a few moments.

"'Unless you change and become like little children, you will never enter the kingdom of heaven'" (Matthew 18:3).

God can do things that seem impossible

Bible stories:
  Creation story—Genesis 1; 2
  Noah's ark—Genesis 6:1–9:17
  Jonah—Jonah 1–4

THINGS YOU NEED:

• scissors
• 2-3 sheets of paper—about 6 x 9 inches (or half an A4 sheet)

Worship activities:
  1. Tell your child that God can do things that seem impossible to us.
  2. Show your child the piece of paper and ask her if she thinks it would be possible to cut a hole in the paper big enough for you to climb through.
  3. She will probably say No!
  4. Cut the paper, following the instructions carefully. (It's a good idea to practice this beforehand!)
    a. Fold the paper in half lengthways, so that it is 3 x 9 inches.
    b. Starting from the long side with the cut edges, make cuts parallel to the short edge of the paper, about 1/2 inch apart (1 cm), that run from the cut edges towards the folded edge, but that stop 1/2 inch (1 cm) from the folded edge.
    c. Turn the paper around and make similar cuts from the folded edge. Make these cuts fall in between the first set of cuts.
    d. Carefully cut through all the folds on the folded edge except the first and last folds at each end.
    e. Unfold the paper. It will form a large, "stretchy" circle. If you accidentally cut the wrong folds, tape the paper back together, or start again.
  5. If your child can manage scissors, let her try this on her own. It may help to draw the cutting lines on the paper for her, to guide her. A larger sheet of paper may also help.
  6. Tell your child that when you first looked at the paper, cutting such a big hole seemed impossible until you knew how to do it.
  7. God does many things that seem impossible to us, but they are easy for God because He knows how to do them.
  8. Pray, thanking God for doing impossible things for us.

16

Another option:

• Perhaps you have other tricks to show your child that look impossible until you know how. Show her a few of these tricks. Books of science tricks often have many simple ideas.

Just for you:

• Do you need a miracle today? Do some aspects of parenting seem impossible to you? What "impossible" thing would you like to ask God to do today? Don't be afraid to ask Him.

" 'All things are possible with God' " (Mark 10:27).

17

God knows things we don't know

Bible stories:
  Noah—Genesis 6:1–9:17
  Joseph and Pharaoh's dreams—Genesis 41:1-40
  Daniel interprets dreams—Daniel 2

THINGS YOU NEED:
- coloring book with "mystery" coloring pictures, in which shapes are colored using a number or symbol code, for example, G = green, B = blue, or 3 = orange.
- crayons

Worship activities:
  1. Tell your child that God knows things we cannot know. He knows everything that will take place before it happens.
  2. Let your child color the picture. If she finds the numbers or symbols hard to match to the colors, use her crayons to put a mark of the correct color in each section of the picture, to help guide her coloring.
  3. At first the picture may look confusing, but as the colors fill in the shapes, the picture is revealed.
  4. We don't know what will happen, but God does, and everything fits into His special picture of us, which we will find out one day.
  5. Pray, thanking God for knowing all kinds of things we don't know.

Another option:
  • Look through the outside end of a kaleidoscope and then through the eyepiece to see how the pattern in the end of the scope looks different. We see things from the outside, but God sees things from the inside.

Just for you:
  • Think back over your life to the things that once seemed confusing but now make sense to you. How has God worked in your life? What areas is He still working on? What does it mean to you that God knows the overall picture He has for your life?

"All the days ordained for me were written in your book before one of them came to be" (Psalm 139:16).

18

God's ways are best for us

Bible stories:
Abram follows God's call—Genesis 12:1-7
Daniel and his friends—Daniel 1
The Ten Commandments—Exodus 20
Solomon's wisdom—Proverbs

THINGS YOU NEED:

- A long ball of string or yarn (wool)
- A small treat for your child

Worship activities:

1. Take the ball of string and lay a trail for your child in your home or garden.

2. Place the treat somewhere along the string, just before the end, so that your child doesn't just run around to look for the end of the string!

3. Tell your child that a treat is hidden for her somewhere.

4. Give your child a choice: go anywhere the child wants to, or follow the string to the treat.

5. Encourage your child to wind the string up neatly as she follows the trail. Winding it around a cardboard tube may be the easiest and safest option.

6. God has promised a special treat for us: to live in heaven forever and ever.

7. We can choose to go our own way, or we can chose to follow God's way.

8. God doesn't want us to go our own way and miss the special things He has prepared for us.

9. Pray that you and your child will always follow God's directions.

Other options:

- Add several treats along the length of the string. God gives us lots of treats, before we even get to heaven!

- Use picture clues. Cut pictures from a catalog to show objects in the house where the next clue is hidden.

Just for you:

- The text below is very encouraging. Write it out somewhere and look at it whenever you need encouragement. Perhaps you could design a poster with this text and create it on your computer. Print extra copies to give away.

- Don't forget to look out for treats God has left for you along the way.

18

*" 'For I know the plans I have for you,' declares the Lord,
'plans to prosper you and not to harm you, plans to give you hope
and a future' " (Jeremiah 29:11).*

19

God likes to give me good gifts

Bible stories:
The gifts of the wise men—Matthew 2:1-12
Mary anoints Jesus—John 12:1-8
Stories of healing and miracles
Spiritual gifts—1 Corinthians 12:1-11

THINGS YOU NEED:

* wrapping paper
* adhesive tape
* four unsuitable "presents" for your child, such as:
  * T-shirt that is too small
  * big book, such as a college textbook
  * after-shave lotion for a girl or hair ribbons for a boy
  * empty candy or cookie box
  * one good present such as a worship video or colorful Bible story book.

Worship activities:
1. Wrap all the gifts attractively and bring them to worship.
2. Talk about the good gifts that God has given you. Your child is a special gift from God! What else has God given you?
3. Give your child the four unsuitable presents to unwrap. Talk about why each present is a silly present for your child and have fun with how crazy the gifts are, so that she isn't upset by the presents.
4. Then give your child the good gift and let her open it.
5. Talk to your child about one of her special talents that you have noticed. Maybe the child smiles and makes others happy, or likes to sing, or can run fast.
6. Explain how God has given the child that gift to make her happy and to share with others.
7. Thank God for knowing the best presents to give us—our family, home, special talents, and so on.

Another option:
* Take your child with you to help you choose a present for someone. Show the child some unsuitable gifts and see if she can recognize that these wouldn't be good gifts. Let your child help you choose a suitable gift.

19

Just for you:

• What are the special gifts God has given to you? How have they added to your pleasure and ministry? How could you use one of your gifts to bless someone else today?

"Every good and perfect gift is from above"
(James 1:17).

20

God is everywhere

Bible stories:
Joseph in prison—Genesis 39:19-23
Jonah—Jonah 2
Apostles in prison—Acts 16:16-40
Psalm 139

THINGS YOU NEED:
• home in which you can play hide-and-go-seek

Worship activities:
1. Talk to your child about God being everywhere at the same time.
2. Go into your kitchen and ask your child where you are. Then ask your child if you can be in the bedroom at the same time as you are in the kitchen. Can your child be in the bathroom at the same time as being in the office or the garage? No.
3. But God can be everywhere.
4. Play hide-and-go-seek. Let your child hide, and then go and look for your child.
5. When you've found your child, explain that even when you don't know where your child is, God always knows!
6. Ask if your child can think of a place where she could hide and God wouldn't be able to find her. There is no such place! God is everywhere.
7. When you pray, thank God for being in all the different places you go together with your child, and thank Him for keeping you safe and watching over you.

Other options:
• Take photos of, or help your child draw, the significant places in your lives, such as church, day care, the stores, a park, or the homes of friends and relatives.
• Draw pictures or use photographs of you and your child, and cut them all out separately.
• Let your child move the pictures of you both from place to place, and then ask the child if God is there in that place too.
• God is there all the time, in every place, wherever we go!

Just for you:
• How does remembering that God is everywhere make a difference in

20

your life? When did you feel nearest to God? When did you feel furthest away?
 • God has always been very close to you, even if there were times when
you felt a long way from Him.

"'And surely I am with you always, to the very end of the age'"
(Matthew 28:20).

God Made My Amazing Body!

Young children are learning all about their bodies and what they can do. They are busy mastering new skills every day.

Our bodies are an amazing gift from God. Even if we have a disability or something we consider to be an imperfection, we are still made in the image of our Creator God.

The following worship activities are based around our different senses and different parts of our body. Enjoy these worships as you and your child explore your amazing bodies. Be filled with wonder and praise for God at the way He has designed us. Discover ways to use your bodies to serve God and share His love.

21

God gave me ears so that I can hear and learn

Bible story:
Samuel hears God's call—1 Samuel 3:1-21

THINGS YOU NEED:

- apron
- table covering
- mixing bowl and wooden spoon
- 1 cup peanut butter
- 1 cup runny honey
- 1 cup of dried milk powder or soy milk powder
- dried coconut
- tiny candy cases
- (use half cups and adjust quantities if you need to)

Worship activities:
1. Tell the story of Samuel listening to God's instructions and obeying them.
2. Have everything ready to make the candies.
3. Cover the table, and put an apron on your child.
4. Explain that listening and obeying keep us safe and happy. People that care for us tell us what to do because they want the best for us.
5. Tell your child that you are going to make some healthy candies together. But you can't do much to help, so you are going to tell him what to do.
6. Tell him the following recipe, one stage at a time.
7. Each time you tell your child what to do, encourage him to repeat the instructions back to you to check that he has heard you correctly.

Peanut Butter Fudge Candies
    a. Wash hands well. Mix together the peanut butter and honey in the big bowl.
       Add the dried milk powder and stir it in with a wooden spoon. (Your child may need help because the mixture can be a bit stiff.)
    b. Mix everything together really well until you can make it into small balls. If it's too sticky, add some extra powder; if it's too stiff, add some extra peanut butter.
    c. Leave the balls as they are, or roll some in coconut.
    d. Place the balls into the candy cases. Wash hands again!

21

8. As you enjoy the candies together, talk about how they came out well because your child listened carefully to your instructions.

Other options:
- Use any other simple activity that has a few easy instructions, such as putting together a simple toy or making a sandwich.
- Make these candies to give as a gift for someone.

Just for you:
- How might God be trying to get your attention so that He can talk to you?
- What do you think He wants to say to you? How can you find the time to listen to Him?
- How can you take the time to really listen to your child today?

"My son, pay attention to what I say; listen closely to my words"
(Proverbs 4:20).

22

God gave me ears so that I can hear beautiful things

Bible story:
Saul listens to David's harp—I Samuel 16:14-23

THINGS YOU NEED:
- short story book
- tape or CD of nature sounds with music, for example, dawn chorus in an English wood or music like Vaughan Williams's "The Lark Ascending"
- earplugs

Worship activities:

1. What beautiful things does your child like to listen to? Ask him to think of the things he likes to hear. It's lovely to hear people tell you that they love you very much and to hear the sounds of your favorite people and animals.

2. What would it be like if you didn't hear very well? Put the earplugs in your child's ears, or ask him to plug his ears with his fingers. Then read some of his favorite story. Hug him and tell him that you love him, and put on some nice music.

3. Then take out the earplugs and let your child hear again.

4. What was it like when everything was quiet and muffled?

5. What are the nice things about hearing a story, hearing loving words, and listening to beautiful sounds?

6. Sit quietly and listen to some of the lovely music for a few moments.

7. Thank God for ears to hear words and sounds!

Another option:
- Go to a place where there are lots of nature sounds, such as a forest, park, aviary, or a beach. Listen to the sounds together and find out what is making the different noises.

Just for you:
- What sounds soothe you? Put on some pleasant music as you drive or work around your home, and enjoy some beautiful sounds. As you listen to the music, imagine yourself curled up next to God, and let Him soothe all the ripples out of your life.

"The birds of the air . . . sing among the branches"
(Psalm 104:12).

23

God gave us ears so that we can make music to praise Him

Bible story:

David makes music—Psalm 150

THINGS YOU NEED:

- musical toys or instruments
- dry, transparent plastic water bottle with screw-on lid
- bits of colored paper, beads, glitter, confetti, etc.
- handful of dried lentils, peas, or rice

Worship activities:

1. King David liked to make music to praise God.

2. He wrote lots of songs as well. Read Psalm 150.

3. Ask your child about his favorite praise songs, and sing them together.

4. Use the instruments and musical toys to accompany the praise song and see how many sounds you can make together.

5. Make your own simple instrument by filling the plastic bottle with the dried pulses and the glitter, etc. The glittery things are to make it look pretty.

6. Use the homemade instrument to accompany your praise songs.

7. Thank God that we can praise Him with lots of lively music!

Another option:

- If you don't have instruments, use a collection of unbreakable kitchen items and let your child have fun clashing pan lids together or using a wooden spoon as a drumstick on a kitchen pot.

Just for you:

- Make a recording of the songs you find the most uplifting so that you can listen to them as you exercise, drive, or work.

*"Praise him with tambourine and dancing,
praise him with the strings and flute, praise him with the clash of
cymbals, praise him with resounding cymbals. Let everything that has
breath praise the Lord" (Psalm 150:4-6).*

24

God gave us ears to keep us safe

Bible story:
The Ten Commandments—Exodus 20

THINGS YOU NEED:
- space for your child to run around

Worship activities:
1. Talk about the importance of ears for helping us listen to what is going on around us.
2. Have your child run around in a garden or park. Every time he hears you call, "Stop!" he should stand absolutely still until you say "Go!" again.
3. Before he gets tired of the game, find a place to sit and talk. Ask your child why you might tell him to stop running. It might be when there is danger, such as when a river is close by, or a busy road.
4. Other warning sounds might be car horns, bicycle bells, emergency vehicle sounds, a barking dog, and a smoke alarm.
5. Thank God for giving us ears to help protect us from danger, so that we can hear the warning sounds and choose to be safe.

Another option:
- Go around the house and listen to all the warning sounds your house can make—such as the buzzer on the dryer, the smoke alarm, the burglar alarm, and the sound the phone makes when it's been left off the hook.

Just for you:
- What warning systems has God built into your body because He loves you and wants to help you stay safe?
- Are you getting any warning sounds at the moment?
- How can you listen to the warnings and respond wisely?

"Listen, my son ... and the years of your life will be many"
(Proverbs 4:10).

25

God gave me a nose so that I can smell lovely things

Bible story:
Mary anoints Jesus' feet—John 12:1-11

THINGS YOU NEED:
- soft scarf for a blindfold
- collection of three nice-smelling things such as:
  - soap, shampoo, perfume, lavender flowers, an orange, vanilla essence, maple syrup, cinnamon
  - scented candle, or some stove-top potpourri

Worship activities:
1. God gave us noses so that we can smell lovely things in the world around us.
2. Blindfold your child and then let him smell the three nice-smelling things. See if he can identify each smell. This may be hard if he is very young, so you could ask him if he likes the smell or not.
3. If you feel it is safe to do so, show your child something you use around the home to make it smell nice, such as an air freshener spray, plug-in room fragrance, scented candle, or stove-top potpourri.
4. Talk together about why it is nice when our home smells good.
5. Thank God for all the lovely smells He has made.

Another option:
- Let your child choose his favorite room fragrance for your home.

Just for you:
- What's your favorite room fragrance? How do you fragrance your home by your actions and words? What beautiful things do you bring to the home atmosphere? How is God like a room fragrance in your life? How can everyone who comes to your home enjoy the fragrance of God's love?

"And the house was filled with the fragrance of the perfume"
(John 12:3).

26

God gave me a nose so that I can smell good things to eat

Bible story:
Jacob makes a stew—Genesis 25:29-34

THINGS YOU NEED:

- ready-to-bake bread or cinnamon buns
- soft scarf to use as a blindfold
- assortment of food and nonfood items that smell good
- some rotten or spoiled food

Worship activities:

1. Put the cinnamon buns or ready-to-bake bread in a hot oven. Set a timer so that you don't forget they are there while you do the rest of the worship activity.

2. Talk about how our noses help us to smell what is good to eat.

3. Blindfold your child and let him smell all the different things you have found. See if he can choose what is good to eat, for example, an orange, and what is not good to eat, for example, shampoo.

4. If you have some food that has spoiled, you might like to let your child smell that too, to show that when food isn't good to eat, it can smell bad.

5. By now the baked goods should smell delicious. Enjoy eating the fragrant foods together.

6. Thank God for foods that smell wonderful.

Other options:

- Do this worship just before breakfast so that you can eat the buns right away without spoiling an appetite.
- Visit a bakery to smell freshly baked goods.

Just for you:

- Is there someone you know who would enjoy some freshly baked goods? Perhaps you could share some with them, or invite a friend over with her family to eat breakfast with you, or meet a friend in a bakery for lunch.
- Things often smell even better when the experience is shared!

" 'Take ... as a gift—a little balm and a little honey, some spices and myrrh, some pistachio nuts and almonds' " (Genesis 43:11).

God gave me eyes so that I can see beautiful things

Bible story:
Creation—Genesis 1; 2

THINGS YOU NEED:
- collection of beautiful natural objects such as flowers, fruit, nuts, and stones.
- soft blindfold

Worship activities:
1. Have the objects ready to use but hidden from your child's sight.
2. Ask your child what he thinks is the most beautiful thing he has ever seen.
3. Blindfold him and explain that you will give him some very beautiful things to feel.
4. Ask your child to describe what he feels. Can he guess what the object is just by touching it? Can he tell how beautiful the object is, or what color it is?
5. Take off the blindfold and let him see the objects.
6. Thank God for making beautiful things for us to see.

Another option:
- Show your child beautiful pictures of nature and scenery. Ask him to choose the picture he likes best, or to tell you which thing in the picture is the most beautiful.

Just for you:
- Perhaps you could buy one beautiful flower today, such as an orchid. Put it where it will remind you of the beautiful things in your world.
- What are the beautiful things that God has put around you to delight you?
- Perhaps you could buy another beautiful flower to give to someone at work, who may be new or in need of cheering up.

"And God saw that it was good" (Genesis 1:10).

God gave me eyes so that I can enjoy all the colors in the world

Bible stories:
God's rainbow—Genesis 9:12-17
Joseph's coat—Genesis 37:1-4

THINGS YOU NEED:
- packet of multicolored candies, buttons, or beads
- muffin pan
- brown paper bag

Worship activities:
1. Show the colored candies, buttons, or beads to your child. Look together at the pretty colors.
2. In the muffin pan, place one red item in one muffin cup, a blue item in another cup, and so on until each color has its own separate muffin cup, identified by the colored object sitting in it.
3. Put the other colored items into the brown paper bag.
4. Ask your child to take a colored item out of the paper bag and to name something that is the same color as the item in his hand.
5. Then let the child put the item in the correct cup, and take another item out of the paper bag.
6. Pray, thanking God for things that are different colors: "I thank You, God, for apples that are red, the water that is blue, soft grass that is green," etc.

Another option:
- Find a large, colorful picture of nature objects, or a countryside scene. Place the colored candies, buttons, or beads on the picture, matching them to the colors on the background.

Just for you:
- What are your favorite colors? Try linking each of your favorite colors with an aspect of God's love. Blue—God washes me clean with the water of His forgiveness; red—Jesus shed His blood for me; green—He gives me fresh new life.

"Open my eyes that I may see wonderful things in your law" (Psalm 119:18).

29

God gave me eyes to see when other people need help

Bible stories:

Jesus feeds five thousand hungry people—Matthew 14:13-21

Jesus washes the disciples' feet—John 13:1-17

THINGS YOU NEED:

- cup half filled with water
- dry dish towel
- hand fan

Worship activities:

1. Place the items on a low table close to where you will do the worship. Do this in a place where it doesn't matter if water spills.

2. Talk about how God gave us eyes so that we can see when other people need help.

3. Jesus was always looking around for people who needed His help.

4. Show your children the cup of water, dish towel, and fan. Show your children how the fan works if they haven't seen one before, and how it creates a cooling breeze. Ask them if they know when a dish towel is needed. Go and sit at a table or counter where you can safely spill something.

5. Pretend to be very hot, tired, and thirsty.

6. Can your children see your needs? If they are not sure how to help you, ask them to look at the objects on the low table for some ideas.

7. Perhaps they could fan you to cool you down, or bring you a drink.

8. When they bring you a cup of water, spill it a little and see if they will bring you the dish towel and help you wipe up the spill.

9. Each time your child helps you, thank them for noticing that you needed help, and for bringing what you needed.

10. Think together of a time when you needed help and Jesus gave you what you needed—money, food, lost keys, etc.

11. Pray, thanking God for noticing when you need help and providing what you need.

Other options:

- Look together at pictures of people needing help. Talk about the kind of help they need.

29

- Mime situations in which you might need your children's help and see if they can guess the kind of help you need.

Just for you:
- Remember a time when someone has noticed your need and helped you. How did that encourage you?
- Is there someone close to you who has a need? Ask them, "If I could do one thing to help you today, what would you like it to be?"
- What one thing would you like God to do for you today? Ask Him for His help too.

"Share with God's people who are in need. Practice hospitality"
(Romans 12:13).

30

God gave me eyes to help me do things

Bible stories:

Isaac blessing Jacob and Esau—Genesis 27:1-40
Jesus heals a blind man—Luke 18:35-43

THINGS YOU NEED:

- one child's large sweater
- one pair of spacious child's pants
- one pair of child's clean shoes
- soft blindfold

Worship activities:

1. Lay your child's clothes out on the floor so that the child can see where they are.

2. Blindfold your child.

3. Ask the child to put on the sweater, pants, and shoes without seeing.

4. Ask your child—what was hard about getting dressed without seeing your clothes?

5. What other things would be very hard to do if you couldn't see?

6. Pray a prayer with open eyes, thanking God that you can see to do the things you need to do. If your child is visually impaired—thank God for giving other people eyes to see so that they can help your child when necessary.

Another option:

- Use a simple wooden jigsaw puzzle with a few pieces. Turn all the pieces upside down and see if you and your child can put together the puzzle without looking at the picture.

Just for you:

- How can you see those around you through eyes of wonder, remembering that they have been made in God's image? Think about the story of the blind man who saw men as trees walking in Mark 8:22-26.
- How do we sometimes see people as trees, to cut down, exploit, and use rather than as people who need to be loved?

"Immediately he received his sight and followed Jesus along the road"
(Mark 10:52).

31

God gave me hands so that I can feel different things

Bible story:
Isaac feeling Jacob's and Esau's arms—Genesis 27:1-40

THINGS YOU NEED:
- variety of different textured surfaces, such as sandpaper, kitchen towel, foil, bubble wrap, fur fabric, felt.
- large paper bag
- white card
- scissors
- stick adhesive

Worship activities:
1. Before worship, put all the different textures into the paper bag.
2. Talk about all the different textures our hands can touch.
3. Let your child put her hand in the bag to feel the different textures.
4. Can she recognize any of the textures by touching them?
5. Pull out all of the textured pieces and help your child make a feely collage. Cut different shapes out of the textures and help your child stick them onto the card.
6. Thank God for making our hands so that we can feel all kinds of different things. In your prayer, thank Him for something soft, something rough, something smooth, and something hard.

Another option:
- Cut the letters of your child's name out of different textures and let them arrange the letters to make her name before sticking the pieces down.

Just for you:
- What parts of your life feel rough, what parts feel smooth, what parts feel cozy and furry, and when do you think you shine?
- How does God use the different textures of your life to bless you?

" 'If I only touch his cloak, I will be healed' "
(Matthew 9:21).

God gave me hands so that I can be helpful

Bible story:
Samuel helping in the temple—1 Samuel 2:18-21

THINGS YOU NEED:

- pencil and paper
- scissors

Worship activities:

1. Talk with your child about the different things people can do with their hands. What does your child do with her hands, starting from when she gets up until when she goes to bed?

2. Help your child draw around her hands on the paper.

3. Talk about the things your child does that you find especially helpful.

4. On each of the drawn fingers, write one thing that your child does to help you.

5. Pray, thanking God for each of the ways your child has helped you that you have written on the paper hands.

6. Cut out the hands and pin them on your bulletin board.

Another option:

- Take the time to teach your child a simple but helpful thing she could do with her hands. Find a way to make the task enjoyable.

Just for you:

- What burdens are you carrying today? Who could share your load? How can you carry someone else's burdens?
- Perhaps you have a friend who also has a burden. Why not swap burdens for a while and carry each other's load for an hour or so by caring for each other's children, giving each other a short break, or by cleaning each other's home?
- It can feel much better when we are helping another person than when we are carrying our own burdens.

"Carry each other's burdens" (Galatians 6:2).

33

God gave me hands so that I can share

Bible stories:
Elijah and the widow of Zarephath—1 Kings 17:7-16
A little boy shares his lunch with Jesus—John 6:1-13

THINGS YOU NEED:
- collection of your child's favorite soft toys or dolls
- several egg cups
- handful of colored buttons, toy bricks, raisins, etc.
- colored card
- hole punch
- scissors, stickers, marker pens
- narrow ribbon or embroidery floss

Worship activities:
1. Ask your child to find her favorite soft toys or dolls and bring them to worship.
2. Ask your child to give each toy an egg cup.
3. Give your child the colored buttons or raisins, and ask her to share the objects between the toys. If she doesn't know how to do this, show her how to place one of each item in each egg cup until they are all given out.
4. Talk about the importance of sharing the special things we have.
5. Make some Bible bookmarks out of the colored card. Write verses on them, loop ribbon or floss through a punched hole, and decorate with stickers.
6. Place the bookmarks in a vase by the front door to give to visitors.
7. Thank God that you have enough things to share with others.

Another option:
- Bake cookies or bread together to share with neighbors.

Just for you:
- What was the nicest thing anyone ever shared with you? Why did it mean so much to you? Who was the first person to share the good news of Jesus with you?

"'Give to the one who asks you, do not turn away from the one who wants to borrow from you'" (Matthew 5:42).

34

God gave me a tongue so that I can taste delicious foods

Bible stories:
> Manna in the wilderness—Exodus 16
> Daniel and the king's food—Daniel 1
> The great banquet—Luke 14:15-24

THINGS YOU NEED:

- six teaspoons
- six different items your child likes to taste, such as honey, peanut butter, applesauce, mashed banana, yogurt, cheese spread

Worship activities:

1. Talk about lots of different flavors that God has created. What are your child's favorite foods? What would it be like if all food tasted the same?

2. Give your child tiny tastes of the different foods and see if the child can guess what the foods are.

3. Which one of these does your child like the best?

4. Which flavors do you like the best?

5. Thank God for tongues to taste all the different flavors.

Another option:

- Do this at a mealtime and cut thin slices of bread into little squares to make miniature sandwiches with six different fillings. See if your child can guess what the different fillings are.

Just for you:

- What's on the "plate" of your life at the moment? What things are you happy to have on your plate? What things would you rather not have on your plate?
- Praise God for the delicious things that are on your plate, and ask Him to help you know what to do with the less tasty things.

"Taste and see that the Lord is good"
(Psalm 34:8).

35

God gave me a tongue so that I can say kind words

Bible stories:
Rebekah is kind to a stranger—Genesis 24
Ruth and Naomi—book of Ruth

THINGS YOU NEED:

* something soft and cuddly, like a teddy bear
* something hard and spiky, like a hard hairbrush or a hammer

Worship activities:

1. Talk to your child about a time when she said some really kind and loving words. Perhaps the child told you she loved you, or thanked you for a meal, or said something that encouraged you. Repeat what your child said and tell how you felt when you heard it.

2. Tell your child that the kind words were like a warm hug from a cuddly bear!

3. Explain that not all words can feel good. Some words are hard and spiky and feel hurtful. Show them the hard and spiky thing.

4. Tell your child that you will say six different things. Some will be warm and kind, and then your child has to pick up the teddy bear. Some will be not such nice words, and then the child needs to pick the hairbrush or hammer.

5. Pray, asking God to help you choose to say things in warm, loving, and encouraging ways.

Other options:

* Use toy bricks to build a small tower or building, leaving out some spare bricks.
* Ask your child to put a brick on the tower every time you say a kind phrase, and to take a brick off the tower every time you say an unkind phrase. Then say two unkind phrases and four kind phrases in any order you like. The tower should be higher by the end of the activity.

Just for you:

* Make a list of ten encouraging Bible promises that build you up. Keep them somewhere where you can look at them often.

"Do not let any unwholesome talk come out of your mouths, but only what is helpful for building others up according to their needs, that it may benefit those who listen" (Ephesians 4:29).

36

God gave me a tongue so that I can praise Him

Bible stories:

Miriam praising God after crossing the Red Sea—Exodus 15:1-21
David praising God—Psalm 148
Children praising Jesus in the temple—Matthew 21:12-17

THINGS YOU NEED:

- box or bag
- objects that remind your child of special things about God, such as:
  - crown—King
  - silk flower—Creator
  - soft toy—loves us
  - toy car—keeps us safe when we drive
  - eraser—forgives us, erases our sins
  - bandage—heals us

Worship activities:

1. Show your child all the objects you have collected.
2. Talk with your child about the different aspects of God that they represent.
3. Put all the objects in a bag or box.
4. Take turns drawing an object out of the box and saying a praise sentence. For example, if you take the soft toy out of the bag, you would say, "I praise You, God, because You love us!"
5. This activity can also be used as a prayer activity.

Another option:

- Set the praise phrases you use to a simple tune and turn this praise activity into a song. Let your child hold up the different objects as she sings to represent different praise phrases.

Just for you:

- Find a collection of objects that represent these aspects of God and arrange them in a collection where you will see them often, on a shelf, on a wooden plate, or even in a box frame to hang on the wall.

"Let everything that has breath praise the Lord" (Psalm 150:6).

37

God gave me feet so that I can come quickly when I am called

Bible stories:
Samuel obeys quickly—I Samuel 3
The disciples follow immediately—Matthew 4:18-22

THINGS YOU NEED:
• house or garden that has places to hide

Worship activities:
1. Cheerfully call your child to come to worship.
2. Talk about the importance of coming quickly when someone you know calls you.
3. Hide somewhere and then call your child to come to you.
4. Repeat the game a couple of times and then swap roles so that your child hides and calls for you.
5. Thank God for feet that can run quickly when they need to.

Another option:
• Make a cardboard shape of a mother chicken or sheep. Make another small shape of a baby chick or lamb. Punch a hole in the middle of each shape. Tie an 18-inch (45-cm) piece of string between the holes in the baby and the mother. Tie it so that when you pull the string through the back of the mother, the baby comes to her quickly. Add more babies if you like.
• Play with this for a little while, talking about how baby animals need to run quickly to their mothers for safety, just like human children.

Just for you:
• How does God call you? What do you do when He calls? Why do you think He might be calling you? What is He calling you to do today?

"Jesus called them, and immediately they left their boat and their father and followed him" (Matthew 4:21, 22).

38

God gave me feet so that I can move around

Bible story:
Peter and John heal the lame man—Acts 3:1-12

THINGS YOU NEED:
- two pillows, preferably different colors, such as pink and blue
- large piece of extra-strong kitchen foil
- bath towel

Worship activities:

1. Think of some questions you could ask your child to which she would answer Yes or No.

2. Tell your child that you will ask some questions, but instead of saying Yes or No, she must run to the blue pillow to answer No, and to the pink pillow to answer Yes.

3. Ask questions and have the child run until she begins to get tired, and then pull up the pillows and sit on them together.

4. Talk about how our feet help us to move around, and how they can take us to the different places that we choose to go.

5. Praise God as you leap and jump together!

Another option:
- Make a fun footprint by folding the bath towel so that it is four layers thick. Place the foil on top of the towel and have your child tread firmly on the center of the foil to make a foil footprint.

Just for you:
- Where are some of the places you like to go? What could you do to show some thoughtfulness and love for other people who also go there? What might Jesus have done to encourage others in your favorite places?

"He went ... into the temple courts, walking and jumping, and praising God" (Acts 3:8).

39

God gave us feet, and we need to take care of them

Bible stories:
Mary anointing Jesus' feet—John 12:1-11
Jesus washing the disciples' feet—John 13:1-17

THINGS YOU NEED:
- scented massage oil or body cream
- tissues

Worship activities:
1. Ask your child to cross the floor of the biggest room in your house without touching the furniture and without putting her feet on the ground.
2. Perhaps the child would roll, or shuffle on her bottom.
3. Our feet work hard for us, even though they are quite small.
4. It's important to look after our feet.
5. Take some special time together as you massage your child's feet with the oil or cream. Let your child massage your feet too.
6. Pray, thanking God for your feet! Perhaps your child could thank God for feet that hop as she hops, for feet that jump as she jumps, and so on through all the activities that feet can do. Prayers can be lively too!

Another option:
- Perhaps you have a foot spa that you can let your child experience, or you could wash your child's feet yourself at a time when they are dirty, or put some of your favorite scent on your child's feet after a bath.

Just for you:
- What could you do to take care of your feet today?
- As you soak, rub, moisturize, and pedicure your feet, take the time to meditate on the story of Mary anointing Jesus' feet. She gave Jesus the very best she had.

"Mary took . . . an expensive perfume; she poured it on Jesus' feet and wiped his feet with her hair" (John 12:3).

40

God made my face special so that people can recognize me

Bible story:

The prodigal son—Luke 15:11-32

THINGS YOU NEED:

- paper
- crayons

Worship activities:

1. Take the paper and pencil and ask your child to try and draw you, while you draw your child. Or try to draw yourselves.

2. When you have finished, look at the pictures side by side. Can you tell which picture is of which person? How can you do this? What is special and unique about each of your faces? Who looks like whom in the family?

3. Tell your child that although we are all different, we are all made in the likeness of God, to show that we are all His children.

4. Thank God for faces so that we can recognize our friends and family members.

Another option:

- Show your child some family photographs. Who can your child recognize? This can be an interesting activity if the photographs are several years old.

Just for you:

- How do you look like your heavenly Father? How can others tell that you are His child? What's one thing can you do today to help someone understand what God is like?

" 'But while he was still a long way off, his father saw him and was filled with compassion for him; he ran to his son, threw his arms around him and kissed him' " (Luke 15:20).

God Made the World!

The story of creation has so much potential for helping children to learn about their world and to discover God's love and creativity. Young children enjoy experiencing stories with their senses, and the Creation story offers many opportunities for multisensory activities.

Some of the most special moments we can spend with a child are when we look together at something beautiful, and see it through their eyes, as though for the very first time. Explore God's world together and share in the wonder of His creation.

41

God made the light so that we can see

Bible stories:
Creation—Genesis 1; 2
The ten virgins—Matthew 25:1-13

THINGS YOU NEED:
- table big enough for you and your child to sit underneath
- several thick, dark blankets to cover the table and hang down to the floor
- child's picture book
- small wooden jigsaw puzzle
- construction toy
  - (Tip: Choose toys that would be difficult to play with in the dark.)

Worship activities:
1. Cover the table with the blankets and make it dark underneath, or find some space in a dark, windowless room or closet.
2. Get into the dark place with your child and the toys.
3. Talk about what the world would be like without light, and before God started to work on His creation.
4. Try to play with the toys in the dark, and then talk about how it feels.
5. What is it like to look at a picture book in the dark, or to do a jigsaw puzzle, or to build something with the bricks? It will be quite hard if you have found a very dark place.
6. Why was it a good idea for God to create light on the first day?
7. What would it be like if this world was dark like night all the time?
8. Pull down the blankets, or turn on the light, and enjoy playing with the toys for a few moments.
9. Praise God for creating light for us!
10. Thank God for light so that we can see.

Other options:
- Blindfold your child, if he doesn't mind, and lead him around the house. Talk about how it would feel to live in darkness all the time.
- When it gets dark early, spend an evening together at home without any lights on. Light safe candles and nightlights and spend a snuggly hour cuddling up and doing something nice. Talk about how the light from the candles makes the darkness more comfortable and fun.

Just for you:

• How has God been a guiding light in your life? What would your life have been like if you had never known God? What kind of light could represent the influence God has in your life at the moment?

"And God said, 'Let there be light,' and there was light"
(Genesis 1:3).

God made the sky

Bible story:
Creation—Genesis 1; 2

THINGS YOU NEED:
- sheets of clear acetate in different colors from an office supplier or craft store
- or colored transparent candy wrappers
- or other colored materials that you can see through easily

Worship activities:
1. Go outside with your child and look at the sky, preferably on a sunny day (but it doesn't matter if it is cloudy).
2. Look at the sky through the different transparent plastics.
3. Talk about what the world would be like if the sky were red all the time, or green, or yellow. Doesn't the world look funny when the sky is a different color? God chose blue because it is the best color for our sky and because it makes our world a prettier place to live in.
4. Thank God for making the sky just perfect, the same way that He has made everything else.

Another option:
- Watch a sunset with your child. Look at all the other pretty colors that appear in the sky as the sun sinks toward the horizon.

Just for you:
- The sky is constantly changing. We are always changing too, even if we can't always see it. In what ways have you changed in the last year? In what ways has your child changed?
- How can you know that God's Spirit is at work in you, just as the wind is forever painting new clouds above us?

"He stretches out the heavens like a tent"
(Psalm 104:2).

God made the clouds

Bible stories:
Noah and the Flood—Genesis 6–8
God's cloud leads the children of Israel—Exodus 13:21, 22

THINGS YOU NEED:
- thick white paper
- white wax crayon or candle
- dilute blue paint
- wide paintbrush
- overalls for child
- protective cloth for table

Worship activities:
1. Create a cloud picture together:
   a. Let your child draw clouds (or just scribble) on the thick white paper with the white wax crayon or candle.
   b. Let him brush blue paint over the paper. The clouds will stay white and show through the blue paint.
   c. Let the painting dry and then write on it: "Thank You, God, for a beautiful sky!"
2. Praise God for beautiful skies!

Other options:
- Use some pink paint as well as the blue and create a sunset picture.
- Make a picture of the sky by tearing long strips of blue tissue paper and gluing them onto a white background. Add some pink and mauve strips at the bottom to make a sunset picture.

Just for you:
- What does your sky look like? What color is your sky at the moment? What kind of sky are you experiencing in your life? What are the clouds like in your sky? Clouds can bring refreshing rain and shade, as well as darkness. Is there something in your clouds that you can be thankful for?
- How is God touching your sky with His paintbrush? What signs of beauty and hope do you see above the horizon?

"The heavens declare the glory of God; the skies proclaim the work of his hands" (Psalm 19:1).

44

God made water to keep us alive

Bible stories:
The Samaritan woman at the well—John 4:1-38
Hagar and Ishmael in the desert—Genesis 21:8-21
Rebekah and the camels—Genesis 24
Water comes from a rock—Exodus 17:1-7

THINGS YOU NEED:

- jug of water
- two clear glass vases or jars
- some flowers from your garden
- a glass of water for each of you

Worship activities:
1. Tell your child that God made water.
2. Let your child place a bunch of flowers in each vase.
3. Help him to pour water into one of the vases, but to leave the other vase dry.
4. Let your child see how quickly the flowers die when they don't have water.
5. Talk about the importance of drinking water because every part of our body needs water to help it work well. Then drink a glass of water together.
6. Pray, thanking God for water to drink so that we stay healthy and refreshed.

Other options:
- Pour two glasses of water. Let your child add some salt to one and taste from both glasses.
- Would your child like to drink salty water all the time? No! God made our water to be sweet, clear, and refreshing for us.

Just for you:
- How can you find ways to "sip" God throughout a busy day? What refreshes you most spiritually, and how can you experience that refreshment more often?

"'Whoever drinks the water I give him will never thirst'" (John 4:14).

45

God made water to keep the world clean

Bible stories:
Naaman—2 Kings 5
Noah's ark—Genesis 6–8
Baptism—Matthew 3:13-17
Jesus washes the disciples' feet—John 13:1-17

THINGS YOU NEED:
• one of your child's toys that needs washing and cleaning
• bowl of warm soapy water and a washcloth
• drying cloth

Worship activities:
1. Prepare a tour of your home to explore places where water is useful for keeping things clean.
2. Talk to your child about water and how we use so much of it to keep ourselves clean.
3. Tell your child that you are going on a hunt to find all the places where water is used to clean things in the home. See if you can guess how many places there might be.
4. Go and find some of these places, and explore them with your child.
5. Help your child wash the toy and make it clean and dry.
6. Thank God for giving us water to help us in so many different ways.

Another option:
• Instead of washing a toy, put your child in the bath when he is obviously dirty, so that the child can see the difference it makes when he is clean again.

Just for you:
• Take a tour of your own life. Which aspects of your life are easy to keep spiritually clean and which aspects are harder to keep clean?
• How does God keep you clean? What is He doing when you are finding it hard to stay clean? Can you keep clean all by yourself? Thank God that He does all the clean-up work necessary!

"Wash me, and I will be whiter than snow"
(Psalm 51:7).

46

God made flowers

Bible stories:
Creation—Genesis 1; 2
God cares for the flowers—Matthew 6:28-30

THINGS YOU NEED:
- some real flowers to look at, in a pot or vase, or in the garden
- green-colored drinking straws
- tissue paper
- colored paper
- scissors
- glue
- paper drinking cup

Worship activities:
1. Look at the real flowers. Talk about the different colors and shapes.
2. Use the tissue and colored paper to create flowers with your child.
3. Let your child design a flower, choosing the color, petals, shape, and leaves.
4. Glue the flowers onto the drinking-straw stems and arrange them in the paper cup.
5. Write on the cup, "Thank You, God, for flowers."
6. Look at the real flowers and compare them with the ones you made together. How are they different and how are they similar?
7. God made thousands of different flowers, in all kinds of ways, to make the earth extra beautiful for us to live in.

Another option:
- Let your child sprout some alfalfa seeds or bean sprouts. These grow quickly, and the child can soon enjoy eating them! Sprout the seeds in a seed sprouter, or in a large jar, and rinse them regularly.

Just for you:
- God cared enough about our world to create thousands of different flowers to decorate it for us. Perhaps you could purchase a flower to remind you of God's love for you, or give one to someone else to brighten their day.

" 'See how the lilies of the field grow. . . . Yet I tell you that not even Solomon in all his splendor was dressed like one of these' "
(Matthew 6:28, 29).

God made fruit for us to eat

Bible stories:
Creation—Genesis 1; 2
Abigail gives fruit to David—1 Samuel 25:18-35
Daniel and his friends—Daniel 1

THINGS YOU NEED:

- large bowl
- some blunt knives
- selection of easy-to-cut fruit such as bananas, peaches, kiwi, and pineapple slices.

Worship activities:
1. Make a fruit salad with your child.
2. As you work together, look at each fruit. See how each is different, with different colors, patterns, textures, and tastes.
3. Take the time to show your child how each fruit is peeled and sliced differently.
4. Let your child help you chop up the fruit in any way he wants to help you make the fruit salad.
5. Thank God for creating such wonderful fruits and flavors for us to eat.
6. Then eat and enjoy!

Another option:
- Blend the fruits to make a smoothie drink instead of a fruit salad, adding fruit juice, milk, or soy milk to achieve the right consistency.

Just for you:
- What kinds of fruit are you producing in your life? If someone looked at your life, would they describe you as an encouragement tree, or a helping tree, or a happy tree? What kind of tree would God call you? What kind of tree do you think God wants you to be?

"The land produced vegetation: plants bearing seed according to their kinds and trees bearing fruit with seed in it" (Genesis 1:12).

48

God made vegetables for us to eat

Bible story:
Daniel and his friends—Daniel 1

THINGS YOU NEED:
- selection of salad vegetables, such as:
  - grated carrots,
  - celery and carrot sticks,
  - and thinly sliced cucumber, peppers, and tomatoes
- plain plate
- plastic wrap

Worship activities:

1. Show your child all the different vegetables that God has made. Look at their different colors, shapes, and textures. Talk about their tastes and which ones you like the best.

2. Let your child make a picture salad using the different vegetables. Perhaps he could make a face out of the vegetables.

3. Or try making a different face-salad for each person in the family.

4. Cover the salads with plastic wrap and keep refrigerated until dinner.

5. Thank God for lots of different vegetables to keep us healthy. Add different adjectives to the vegetables in your prayers: "Thank You, God, for crunchy carrots, crinkly lettuce, springy sprouts, cool cucumbers, and perky peppers!"

Another option:
- In winter you might like to make a stew or soup instead of a salad. Let your child help you prepare the vegetables and add them to the stew.

Just for you:
- Think about the text below. List the things that you appreciate about your family members. Perhaps you could create a really simple but tasty meal of vegetables and have a special time of sharing appreciation for each other.

*"**Better a meal of vegetables where there is love than a fattened calf with hatred**" (Proverbs 15:17).*

49

God made plants with seeds and nuts

Bible stories:
Daniel and his friends—Daniel 1:3-21
The parables of the sower, weeds, and mustard seeds—Matthew 13:1-43

THINGS YOU NEED:
- recipe for granola or muesli
- ingredients for the recipe
- big bowl, spoon, and measuring cup

Worship activities:
1. Talk to your child about all the seeds and nuts that God has made for us to eat.

2. Ask your child to help you make the granola or muesli. Show the child the nuts, seeds, and grains that you are using to make the recipe. See how they are all different.

3. Talk about how different seeds grow into different things. Some grow into helpful plants, whose seeds we can eat. Some seeds grow into weeds that aren't helpful to us.

4. Thank God for seeds, nuts, and grains that help make us big and strong.

Another option:
- Go for a walk in the countryside, or a park, and look for all kinds of seeds—floating seeds, spinning seeds, sticky seeds, tiny seeds, etc.

Just for you:
- Think about the different people who planted seeds of God's love in your life. What seeds could you choose to represent their influence in your life? Some seeds are large and noticeable, others are small and fragile. Some blow around in the wind and come and go; others stick with you.

"Other seed fell on good soil, where it produced a crop—a hundred, sixty or thirty times what was sown" (Matthew 13:8).

50

God made different trees with different leaves

Bible story:
Zacchaeus—Luke 19:1-9

THINGS YOU NEED:

- packet of air-drying clay
- small rolling pin
- collection of tree leaves with pronounced veins on their undersides
- drinking straw
- blunt knife
- baking parchment
- coat hanger
- green yarn
- green paint

Worship activities:

1. Collect a few different tree leaves.

2. Help your child to roll out the air-drying clay to a quarter-inch (1/2-cm) thickness.

3. Then let him lay a leaf, vein side down, on the air-drying clay and roll a rolling pin firmly over the leaf. When he lifts up the leaf, the pattern of its veins should remain on the clay.

4. Cut around the edges of the leaf shape with a blunt knife to make a clay leaf shape with a vein pattern imprint.

5. Use a drinking straw as a cutter and press it into the clay at the base of the leaf to make a neat round hole in the clay leaf, so that it can be hung up.

6. Let the leaves dry. Then paint them green, or fall colors, and hang them with green yarn from the coat-hanger to make a leaf mobile.

7. Thank God for making all the different trees with their different leaves.

Another option:

- Lay the leaves, vein side up, on a table, and place a sheet of thin white paper over the leaves. Roll unwrapped wax crayons across the paper, so that the vein patterns are revealed on the paper. Cut these leaves out and make a mobile or a collage.

50

Just for you:

• Leaves are the power source of trees. They use the light from the sun to transform what is inside of them. What is your power source? How can you maximize your exposure to the Son of God and feel His influence in your life?

"And the leaves of the tree are for the healing of the nations"
(Revelation 22:2).

51

God made trees for us to use

Bible story:
Jesus is a carpenter—Mark 6:1-6

THINGS YOU NEED:
- collection of items made from wood, wood pulp, or other tree products, such as paper, cardboard boxes, maple syrup, cork, wooden items, nuts, and fruits.

Worship activities:
1. Talk about all the different ways that we can use trees. Show your child the different things you have found that come from trees.
2. Walk around your home together, looking for all the things made from tree products.
3. Talk together about what it would be like without trees and all the things they give us. How would we build our houses, make furniture, print books, etc.? Many things come from trees!
4. Thank God for creating trees to be so useful to us.

Another option:
- Make something out of a tree product with your child. Perhaps you could put together a simple wooden kit, or decorate a wooden item. Or maybe you would like to make pancakes together and eat them with maple syrup.

Just for you:
- If Jesus could make something for you out of wood, what would you like Him to make?

"He is like a tree planted by streams of water, which yields its fruit in season and whose leaf does not wither. Whatever he does prospers"
(Psalm 1:3).

God made the stars, part 1

Bible stories:
God's promise to Abraham—Genesis 22:15-18
The wise men follow the star—Matthew 2:1-12

THINGS YOU NEED:

- warm clothes
- waterproof groundsheet or tarpaulin and warm blankets to lie on
- children's book about stars and constellations

Worship activities:
1. Do this at a time of year when it gets dark fairly early so that your child doesn't have to stay up too late.
2. Dress up warmly and lie outside under the stars with your child.
3. See if you can help your child find one or two constellations.
4. Perhaps you will even see a shooting star! Look on the Internet to find out when you are most likely to see them.
5. Be filled with wonder as you look at the stars together, and praise God for making them so pretty.

Another option:
- Visit a planetarium with your child. Check before you go whether it has a minimum entry age.

Just for you:
- When you look at the stars in the sky, and remember that God made them all, how do you want to respond to Him?
- The God who made such massive things, in such a measureless universe, cares intimately about you. How do you feel about Him?

"And God said, 'Let there be lights in the expanse of the sky to separate the day from the night' " (Genesis 1:14).

53

God made the stars, part 2

Bible story:
Creation—Genesis 1; 2

THINGS YOU NEED:

- black paper
- adhesive stars
- pencil

Worship activities:

1. Talk about how God made the stars and chose where each one would go in the sky.

2. The God who made the stars and gave them each a special place also knows your child and has put her in just the right place in the world!

3. Give your child a piece of black paper and a sheet of adhesive stars.

4. Help your child make a constellation of stars that spell her name, or the first letter of her name, depending on her ability.

5. Make little marks with a pencil to show your child where to stick the stars if she needs extra guidance.

6. Thank God for putting each star in its special place, and for putting your child into the special place in your home.

Another option:

- Instead of marking the black paper with a pencil, use a thick needle to make holes in the black paper where your child needs to stick stars. Then stick the papers on a window, so that light shines through the holes, helping your child see where to stick her stars.

Just for you:

- The God who hung the stars in the sky in their perfect places has put your child in your family, in the perfect place for her.
- God has put you right where you are for a purpose. How are you discovering His purpose for you and your child?

"The heavens are the work of your hands"
(Psalm 102:25).

54

God made the sun

Bible stories:
The sun stands still—Joshua 10:1-15
Jonah and the sun—Jonah 4:5-11

THINGS YOU NEED:

- sunny day
- some flat pebbles or buttons to use as markers
- stick—about two feet long (60 cm)
- plastic beaker to place upside down on top of the stick
- mallet to knock the stick into the ground
- clock that can be set to ring every hour

Worship activities:

1. Talk to your child about the importance of the sun. What does it do? It gives us light and warmth, but it also helps the plants to grow. Sunlight is good for our health in small, safe doses. But it isn't good for our eyes.

2. Do a small experiment to show how the sun moves in the sky so that we can tell the time.

3. Pound the stick into a safe place in your garden, with plenty of clear space surrounding it. Place the beaker over the end to keep your child safe.

4. Tell your child that every hour you will both come out and see how the stick's shadow has moved.

5. As the clock rings at each hour, take the beaker off the stick and place a marker (e.g., stone, popsicle stick) on the tip of the stick's shadow.

6. Show your child how the shadow moves throughout the day as the sun moves across the sky.

7. Tell your child how people used to tell the time by the position of the sun.

8. Thank God for all the amazing things that the sun does. Without the sun there would be no life on the earth.

Other options:

- Find out how to make a small paper sundial and use that instead of the stick. If you don't have a garden, you can do this on a sunny windowsill instead, with a short stick and a big piece of paper on which to mark the shadows.

- Go to a park or garden center and find a sundial. See if it has the right time on it. Remember that sundials don't account for human beings turning the clocks forward in the summer!

54

Just for you:

• What are the bright parts of your life? What are the parts that feel warm? Where is there growth in your life and where is there light?

• What about the shadows in your life? How can the warmth of God's love reach into the dark, cold corners of your life?

"God made two great lights—the greater light to govern the day and the lesser light to govern the night" (Genesis 1:16).

God made the birds and fish

Bible stories:
Elijah and the ravens—1 Kings 17:1-6
Jonah and the great fish—Jonah 2

THINGS YOU NEED:

* list of birds and fish, and some of their sounds or actions that your child might know, for example, chicken—say "cluck cluck" and flap bent arms like wings; whale—make the sound and action of spray coming out of the blow hole

Worship activities:
1. Talk to your child about how God fills the skies and the seas with creatures.

2. Ask your child to tell you all the fish and birds she can think of. Then play this game:
    a. Practice the actions and sounds for each bird and fish with your child.
    b. Then call out the name of a fish or bird and let your child do the actions on her own. Have fun together imitating the creatures.

3. Praise God for all the birds and fish He has made, and thank Him for sending the birds to sing to us and put music in our skies.

4. Sing a praise song with your child and thank God that we can sing praises to Him just like the birds do!

Another option:
* Go with your child outside to a quiet place and be very still for a few minutes. How many different bird songs can you hear?

Just for you:
* What praise song, chorus, or hymn is your spiritual theme tune? Why is it so important to you?

"And God said, 'Let the water teem with living creatures, and let birds fly above the earth across the expanse of the sky'" (Genesis 1:20).

God made the animals

Bible stories:
  Creation—Genesis 1; 2
  Noah's ark—Genesis 6–8

THINGS YOU NEED:
• lots of your child's cuddly animal toys (or small plastic toys)
• a big bag such as a garbage bag, or a box

Worship activities:
  1. Tell your child how God created all kinds of animals, and how He let Adam give all the animals their names.
  2. Hide all the toys in a bag or box and bring them out one at a time to show your child.
  3. Let her choose a name for each toy animal. These names can be anything at all. The funnier the better!
  4. Praise God together for all the different kinds of animals that God created.
  5. Thank God for all the animals He has made, to make us laugh and to make the world more interesting.

Another option:
• Invite your child to design a new animal and give it a name. Where will it live? What will it eat? What special things will it do? Perhaps you could try making it out of chenille pipe-cleaners.

Just for you:
• Which of the animals fascinates you the most? Why do you like it so much? What would you have called it if you were Adam? Which animal would you most like to have as a pet in heaven?

"Now the Lord God had formed out of the ground all the beasts.... He brought them to the man to see what he would name them; and whatever the man called each living creature, that was its name"
(Genesis 2:19).

God made us all different

Bible story:
Creation—Genesis 1; 2

THINGS YOU NEED:
- homemade or purchased plain gingerbread people cookies
- small tubes of colored frosting
- different edible cookie decorations

Worship activities:
1. Talk about how God made us all different. If we were all the same, how would we recognize each other? Life is much more interesting when we are all different!

2. Let your child decorate the gingerbread people in different ways, using whatever frosting and decorations she chooses.

3. Look together at how different the cookies are, and enjoy the differences.

4. Spend some time appreciating your child for her God-created uniqueness.

5. Pray for your child, thanking God for her unique gifts. Encourage your child to pray for some people she knows who are different from her.

Another option:
- Use peanut butter, nuts, raisins, grated carrot, and alfalfa (for hair), with cucumber slices, celery slices, tomato, and other foods to create faces on crackers, toasted English muffins, or burger buns.

Just for you:
- How can you get to know someone who is different from you? How can you show your appreciation of their differences?
- How can you appreciate the uniqueness of each person in your family?

"God created man in his own image" (Genesis 1:27).

58

God made us to look after His world

Bible story:
Adam and Eve in the Garden of Eden—Genesis 1; 2

THINGS YOU NEED:

- piece of paper
- crayons and art materials
- sheet of acetate
- permanent marker

Worship activities:

1. Invite your child to create a work of art. Perhaps the child could draw a beautiful garden with lots of colors. Encourage her to do her very best.

2. In the meantime, scribble on the acetate sheet with the permanent marker to make a messy looking mark.

3. When your child has finished the picture, admire the picture and talk about it together. Tell your child that she has done a wonderful job.

4. Then lay your sheet of acetate over the top of the picture.

5. Ask your child how the picture looks now. Does it still look good, or has it been spoiled? Would your child like it if you pinned the picture on the wall and left the messy acetate over the top?

6. God made a beautiful garden, the best ever. It was very beautiful when He finished, but people have spoiled it. It is still very beautiful underneath, but people scribble on God's picture when they leave their garbage in the wrong places.

7. What other things do people do that make God's world look messy?

8. Take the acetate off the picture and tell your child that God is making a new world for us to live in, where everyone will help the world to stay lovely and no one will spoil it.

9. Pray, thanking God for a special place you go to with your child that still looks very beautiful, and thanking Him for making a new world for us to live in one day.

Another option:

- Adopt a small piece of world near to you, and spend time making it more beautiful.

58

Just for you:
  • How can you make your world, or someone else's world, more beautiful today?

"The Lord God took the man and put him in the Garden of Eden to work it and take care of it" (Genesis 2:15).

59

God makes everything beautiful

Bible stories:
> Creation—Genesis 1; 2
> Esther—book of Esther
> Joseph—Genesis 37; 39–48

THINGS YOU NEED:

- child's scrapbook with a plain cover
- or a cylindrical cookie or potato chip tube that is the right size to become a pencil pot
- pile of interesting paper scraps
- scissors
- glue stick
- transparent, protective plastic with adhesive backing

Worship activities:

1. Give your child the plain-looking book or tube.

2. Provide an interesting selection of papers and the glue stick, and let the child cover the whole tube or book cover with the paper scraps so that the book or tube looks attractive.

3. Use the transparent plastic sheet to cover the book or tube, to protect the paper and add an attractive sheen.

4. Admire your child's work and talk about how she transformed something ordinary into something beautiful.

5. Talk about how the world was very plain and ordinary until God made it beautiful with His creation.

6. Thank God for making ordinary things beautiful, and caring enough to create a beautiful world.

Another option:

- If you have time for a longer activity one day, create a model garden in a shoebox or other sturdy box with low sides.

Just for you:

- What are the beautiful things God has done in your life? Perhaps you could draw your life like the design for a garden. What kind of water feature is refreshing you? Where can you find shade and shelter? Which parts of your life do you think are the most beautiful? What flower might be planted in those areas? Which are the areas that need weeding, or that are still bare earth and waiting to be transformed? Invite God to be the Gardener in your life's garden.

"And God saw all that he had made, and it was very good"
(Genesis 1:31).

60

God made a day to rest

Bible stories:
Creation—Genesis 1; 2
The Ten Commandments—Exodus 20

THINGS YOU NEED:

- open space in the home, or out in the garden or a park (if you have a limited space, do all the activities on the spot)
- refreshing drink of water and a comfortable place to sit

Worship activities:

1. Help your child to understand the importance of a day of rest, and how it shows God's love for us.

2. Tell your child that you are going to imagine a whole week of work and activity.

3. Each day there will be a different activity for you to do together.
   a. First day—hop on one leg the entire distance or for about a minute
   b. Second day—run the distance or on the spot for a minute
   c. Third day—jump with both feet for a minute
   d. Fourth day—make windmills in the air with both arms for a minute
   e. Fifth day—do star jumps for a minute
   f. Sixth day—stretch up high and then curl up small, repeat for a minute
   g. Seventh day—at last a day of rest! Sit down comfortably and have a refreshing drink of water together.

4. Thank God that He took care of our need to rest, even though He never gets tired. He gives us a day to rest because He loves us.

Just for you:

- How can you create a Sabbath day of rest in your busy week? How can you make a day in which you can grow closer to family, to friends, and to God? What things would make a restful day enjoyable for your children?

"And God blessed the seventh day and made it holy, because on it he rested from all the work of creating that he had done"
(Genesis 2:3).

Worships for Special Times

Advent and Easter are both special times of celebration when we can take the time to remember the important Bible stories of Jesus' birth, death, and resurrection.

As Christians we have different emphases at these times than those in the commercial and secular worlds. To help our children value these special Bible stories, understand their significance, and experience them from a Christian perspective, we need to nurture their delight by providing unique worship activities.

Families also have other significant moments. There are birthdays and thanksgivings, illnesses and house moves, and temporary absences.

This collection of worships will provide you with some creative ideas to mark these special moments, and to help your child begin to understand the spiritual significance of these seasons and events.

61

The "Gift of Love" heart

Bible story:
The gifts of the wise men—Matthew 2:1-12

THINGS YOU NEED:
- a large sheet of stiff red card
- a packet of thirty-one very small envelopes from a craft store
- scissors
- glue
- marker pen

Worship activities:
1. Prepare the calendar by cutting out a very large red heart from the cardboard.
2. Write the numbers 1 to 31 on the envelopes and arrange them all over the heart, checking that they all fit within the outline. You may need to overlap the envelopes, or even stick some on the back of the heart.
3. Perhaps God sent the wise men to Jesus so that they could give Him gifts to help His family as Mary and Joseph traveled far away from home with very little money.
4. Every day through December, or any other month, let your child place a coin in one of the envelopes on the heart.
5. When every envelope is full, let your child empty out all the money and help you add it up.
6. Let your child go with you to take the money to a charity, or to buy a gift for a needy child or family, or take it to church for a special project offering.
7. Thank God that you have enough money to share with others.
8. Pray with your child for the family or project you are supporting.

Another option:
- Your child could do little jobs in the home to earn money each day for the "Gift of Love" envelopes.

Just for you:
- Each day, look for the things God gives you and write them in your diary.

"'Freely you have received, freely give'"
(Matthew 10:8).

Special gifts

Bible stories:
Rebekah's engagement presents—Genesis 24
The gifts of the wise men—Matthew 2:1-12

T H I N G S   Y O U   N E E D :
* old catalogs or magazines
* scissors
* glue stick
* several sheets of white card
* gift ribbons and gift tags
* marker pens

Worship activities:
1. Fold the white card sheets in half to make large greeting cards.
2. Talk about the importance of giving each other good and thoughtful presents. God always gives us just the right presents.
3. What presents would your child like to give to the other members of the family, if he could give them anything at all?
4. Encourage your child to think about what the recipient likes, is interested in, hopes for, needs, etc.
5. Find pictures of the gifts in the catalogs, where possible, or let your child draw the gifts if you can't find the right pictures.
6. Stick the pictures of the gifts inside the cards with a message: "If only I could I would give you a _____."
7. When the glue is dry, tie the card with gift ribbon as though it were a gift and add a gift tag with the recipient's name on it.
8. Give these special gifts at a family worship time, celebration meal, or gift exchange.
9. Thank God for the good gifts He has given to your family.

Another option:
• Do this activity with a whole family group together. It can be very encouraging to hear what others would like to give you if they could, even if they can't. It really can be the thought that counts!

Just for you:
• If you could give your child just one gift in the whole world, what would

62

you like it to be? What do you think are the most important gifts you could give that will help him in his life?

" 'If you, then, though you are evil, know how to give good gifts to your children, how much more will your Father in heaven give good gifts to those who ask him!' " (Matthew 7:11).

63

A nativity picture box

Bible story:
The birth of Jesus—Luke 2:1-40

THINGS YOU NEED:

- a shoe box
- a pile of old Christmas cards
- double-sided adhesive tape
- adhesive tape
- scissors
- yellow drinking straws or real straw

Worship activities:
1. Tell your child the story of the birth of Jesus.
2. Cut down two adjacent corners of the shoe box so that one long side of the box becomes a flap. Fold this flap in half lengthways to form a long roof.
3. Lay the box down on its uncut long side and trim the two short sides at an angle toward the roof.
4. If any of this cutting has destabilized the box, restick it with adhesive tape.
5. Lay double-sided adhesive tape on the roof section and cover it with straw or yellow drinking straws, cut to size, to make a thatched roof.
6. Cut figures out of the Christmas cards to create your own nativity scene. Be sure to cut an inch-long flap at the base of the figure so that it can be glued in position with the double-sided tape.
7. Arrange the figures in the box and glue them in place.
8. Thank God for sending Jesus as a special present to the earth.

Another option:
- Use a purchased nativity set and let your child add one figure a day. As each figure is added, tell your child about the role of that character in the Bible story.

Just for you:
- Think about the nativity story from the perspective of the different characters. What new insight does that offer you?

" 'Do not be afraid. I bring you good news of great joy that will be for all the people. Today in the town of David a Savior has been born to you; he is Christ, the Lord. This will be a sign to you: You will find a baby wrapped in cloths and lying in a manger' " (Luke 2:10-12).

64

Secret acts of love

Bible story:
Jesus' birth—Luke 2:1-40

THINGS YOU NEED:
- red or white paper cut into heart shapes about four inches (10 cm) across
- marker pen

Worship activities:
1. Write on each heart-shaped piece of paper "Secret act of love."
2. Explain to your child what the words say.
3. Talk about all the kind things you can do for each other as a family, such as helping to clear the table, putting shoes away, tidying up, or picking a bunch of flowers.
4. Help your child to think of a few things he can safely do to help others in the home.
5. Pile all the hearts in a basket and invite your child to put a heart in the place where they have performed a secret act of love.
6. Thank God for all the secret acts of love He does for us. Can you notice where He has been, even though He doesn't leave a paper heart behind?

Another option:
- Put out one basket for each person in the family. Label each basket with a person's name. Place the hearts in another basket. Whenever family members notice that someone else has done something loving and kind, they place a heart in that person's basket.

Just for you:
- Could you do a secret act of love for someone you know today?
- Look out for God's secret acts of love for you.

"This is how God showed his love among us: He sent his one and only Son into the world that we might live through him" (1 John 4:9).

"God loves you" mobile

Bible story:
Jesus' birth—Luke 2:1-40

THINGS YOU NEED:

- red and white card
- marker pen
- scissors
- pencil
- glue stick
- thread

Worship activities:

1. Fold one piece of card in half and draw half a heart on the fold. Cut it out and then open up the heart to check the shape. Refold and cut until you have a good heart shape.

2. Using the heart as a pattern, cut out four red hearts and two white hearts all the same size and shape.

3. Lay one red heart, one white heart, and then one red heart on the table so that they are in a line, one above the other, with the point of one heart pointing to the central dip in the next heart.

4. Apply adhesive to the backs of all of these hearts and lay a length of thread down the middle of the hearts. The top end of the thread should be twelve inches (30 cm) higher than the top of the top heart, and there should be three inches (7 cm) length of thread between the hearts.

5. When all the thread is in the right place, glue a matching heart on top of each of the first hearts. The hearts should hang in a line, one beneath the other.

6. Press hard to make sure the glue sticks, and leave to dry.

7. Write "God" on the top red heart, "Loves" on the white heart, and "You" on the last red heart. Or write these words lightly in pencil and let your child write over the top with a marker pen.

8. Let your child decorate the hearts and give the heart mobile to someone who needs some encouragement.

9. Pray, thanking God that He loves each one of us so much.

Other options:

- Make one big red heart and stick a smaller white heart in the center of the red heart.

65

• Write a love message in the middle of the heart. Use heart stickers to decorate the heart.

Just for you:

• Make a love card to send to God. What would you write in it? What do you think God would write in a love card to you?

• Look at <http://www.fathersloveletter.com> and then email a message to a friend.

"God is love" (1 John 4:16).

66

Jesus is the Light of the world

Bible stories:
The parable of the ten virgins—Matthew 25:1-13
Jesus is the Light of the world—John 1:1-9; 8:12

THINGS YOU NEED:

- flashlight with battery
- empty jar with smooth sides
- scraps of different-colored tissue paper
- PVA adhesive
- water
- bowl
- child's paintbrush
- sand or salt
- tea light

Worship activities:
1. Talk to your child about light and darkness. What would it be like to live in the dark all the time? What would be difficult if you lived in the dark?
2. When we know Jesus, it's as though we are connected with Him and our light can shine. People find out what Jesus is like by the way His friends live.
3. Show your child the flashlight with the battery taken out. See if your child can turn it on. Without the battery, the light won't shine.
4. Put the battery in and let your child turn the flashlight on. Now it will shine. When we are Jesus' friend, He is like our battery, and our light can shine.
5. Make a special candle holder:
   a. Tear the tissue into small pieces.
   b. Dilute the PVA adhesive with water until it is as runny as fresh cream.
   c. Paint the jar with this adhesive mixture and then stick the pieces of tissue paper on the jar, overlapping them slightly at the edges.
   d. Once the jar is covered with tissue, leave it to dry.
   e. Paint over all the tissue paper with another coat of diluted PVA to protect it.
   f. When the jar is dry, pour some salt or sand into the bottom of the jar, place a tea light inside, and then use the jar as a decorative lantern.

66

6. Always be sure that the lantern is safe, and never leave it unattended. Be careful not let your child touch it when the candle is lit.

Another option:
• If your child is safe with electrical appliances, you could use a small lamp, or nightlight, and show how it cannot light up unless it is plugged into the wall socket.

Just for you:
• What is your battery like at the moment—full, half empty, running on reserve? What recharges you: people, creativity, exercise, nature, Bible study? How does God help you top up your batteries?

" 'I am the light of the world. Whoever follows me will never walk in darkness, but will have the light of life' " (John 8:12).

Note: Explaining the story of Jesus' death and resurrection can be a challenge. These concepts are quite difficult even for grown-ups. Here are some activities that families have used to try to explain the story to their children.

The story of Jesus' death

Bible story:

Jesus' death and resurrection—Matthew 26–28; Mark 14:32-72; 15; Luke 22:39-71; 23; 24; John 18–20

THINGS YOU NEED:

- set of building blocks that connect firmly together
- small plastic people

Worship activities:

1. Tell your child a simple story of Jesus' death on the cross and His resurrection. As you tell the story, work together to build a scene:

    a. Build a hill out of bricks, but leave a cave in the side of the hill big enough for a plastic person to lie inside.

    b. Make three crosses out of the bricks and stand them on top of the hill.

    c. Tie three of the people onto the crosses. If you have enough figures, use some to be Jesus' disciples and the soldiers.

    d. Let Jesus' friends take Him off the cross after He has died and place Him in the cave. Make a big stone out of bricks to cover the front of the cave.

    e. Explain how angels came and rolled the stone away, and how Jesus came back to life.

    f. Jesus' friends were so happy to see Him alive again!

2. We're also very happy that Jesus is alive so that we can be with Him forever one day.

3. Pray a happy, thankful prayer that Jesus is alive.

Another option:

- Build the scene with stones, modeling clay, popsicle-stick crosses, and cardboard cut-outs of people.

Just for you:

- Jesus has given us the gift of eternal life! That's the most amazing gift anyone can ever give. How would you like to respond to the offer of such a gift? Write a list of ten things you would like to do in eternity.

"The gift of God is eternal life in Christ Jesus our Lord"
(Romans 6:23).

68

Happy moments, sad moments

Bible stories:

Jesus' death and resurrection—Matthew 26–28; Mark 14:32-72; 15; Luke 22:39-71; 23; 24; John 18–20

Jairus's daughter—Luke 8:49-56

Widow's son—Luke 7:11-17

Lazarus—John 11:38-44

THINGS YOU NEED:

- two circles of colored card
- double-sided adhesive tape
- popsicle stick
- marker pen

Worship activities:

1. Draw a simple sad face on one card circle and a simple happy face on the second card circle.

2. Stick the two circles back to back with a popsicle stick handle in between the two faces, so that both the faces are the right way up when the handle is held like a popsicle.

3. Tell your child the story of Jesus' death in a simple and gentle way. Invite him to show you how the disciples felt when Jesus was on the cross, and when He died and was buried, by showing you the sad face on the stick puppet.

4. When Jesus was resurrected, how did their faces change?

5. Let your child show you the happy face.

6. Explain that Jesus has turned all our sad faces into happy faces because He died for us so that we can live forever.

7. Thank God for making our sad faces happy.

Another option:

- Let your child use his own face to make the sad and happy expressions of the disciples. Perhaps the child would like to add other facial expressions and gestures to illustrate the way the disciples were feeling.

Just for you:

- Think of a time when God turned your sadness into happiness. What happened? Do you have other sadness that you would like God to transform for you? Invite God to perform another "sad into happy" miracle for you.

" 'I am the resurrection and the life. He who believes in me will live, even though he dies' " (John 11:25).

69

Resurrection tree

Bible story:

The story of the Resurrection—Matthew 28; Mark 16; Luke 24; John 20

THINGS YOU NEED:

- sturdy vase
- collection of budding twigs to make an attractive spray in the vase
- torn white cloth strips to tie in bows on the twigs
- spices (for example, cinnamon bark, nutmeg seeds) tied with string or ribbon
- small stones to arrange around the base of the vase
- water for the vase

Worship activities:

1. Tell your child that Jesus died, but He came back to life so that we can go to heaven with Him one day.

2. Explain that we are very happy that Jesus was resurrected. All of Jesus' friends were happy when He rose from the dead too.

3. Jesus' friends went to do special things to His body, with linens and spices, but when they got there, He was already alive!

4. You and your child could go together to look for some nice branches to use for your resurrection tree.

5. Place them in a vase and arrange the stones around the base. The little stones remind us of the big stone that was rolled away from the cave where His body was kept.

6. Talk about how He was wrapped in white cloths, and tear the white cloth into strips. Tie lengths of the cloth onto the twigs in bows. We are happy that the linen wasn't needed when Jesus came back to life.

7. Tie the spices onto the twigs. We are glad that the women didn't need to use the spices that they had prepared to go on His body.

8. Add water to the vase to keep the twigs alive.

9. Thank God that Jesus was brought back to life so that we can live forever one day.

Another option:

- At Advent time, create an Advent tree. Use twigs, evergreen branches, or a small potted evergreen tree. Decorate it with symbols from the nativity story, such as stars, straw ornaments, angels, sheep, and gold decorations. Tell your child the story of Jesus' birth, and each time you mention one of the symbols, let your child hang it on the tree.

69

Just for you:

• Imagine you were one of Jesus' followers on the day of His resurrection. How would you respond to the news that Jesus had risen from the dead?

" 'He is not here; he has risen' " (Matthew 28:6).

70

From death to life

Bible stories:

The resurrection of Lazarus—John 11:38-44

The resurrection of Jesus—Matthew 28; Mark 16; Luke 24; John 20

THINGS YOU NEED:

- bowl of flowering spring bulb plants
- dry bulbs

Worship activities:

1. Show the spring flowers to your child. Look at their beautiful colors and shapes.

2. Which flowers does your child like the best? Which ones do you like the best?

3. Show your child some dry bulbs and explain that when the bulbs are buried in the ground they come to life and grow beautiful flowers.

4. Jesus was dead, and He was buried, but He came back to life even more wonderful than before, just like the bulbs.

5. Because Jesus died, He can bring us back to life again, even more beautiful and wonderful than ever.

Another option:

- Visit a park or bulb field with your child to see the colorful spring plants.

Just for you:

- What does Jesus' resurrection mean to you, personally? How could you remember this in a special way with your family?

"He has made everything beautiful in its time"
(Ecclesiastes 3:11).

Thank You, God!

Bible stories:
Ruth gleaning in the fields—Ruth 2:1-23
The leper who said "Thank You"—Luke 17:11-19

THINGS YOU NEED:

* tray
* seasonal decorations

Worship activities:

1. Harvest and Thanksgiving provide a good time to say "Thank You" to God for everything He gives us.

2. Talk to your child about all the things for which you are thankful.

3. Ask your child what she would most like to thank God for.

4. Help your child collect some items that represent the things she would like to thank God for.

5. Help your child arrange all these things into a centerpiece on the tray.

6. Add seasonal decorations, such as leaves and fruits.

7. At a special meal, invite your child to show what she chose and to say why she chose those items.

8. Thank God for all His special gifts to us.

Another option:

* Collect small things from each family member that represent something in the last year that they want to thank God for, and invite everyone to share their stories of thankfulness at a special meal.

Just for you:

* What new things can you thank God for about your children? Sit your children in your lap and tell them twenty things about them for which you want to thank God.

"Give thanks to the Lord, for he is good; his love endures forever"
(Psalm 106:1)

Thanksgiving placemats

Bible stories:

Manna in the wilderness—Exodus 16
Ruth gleaning in the fields—Ruth 2:1-23

THINGS YOU NEED:

- sheets of thin card
- marker pen or computer and printer
- magazine pictures of food
- glue stick
- transparent adhesive covering film
- laminator

Worship activities:

1. Create Thanksgiving placemats with your child:
   a. Write "Thank You, God!" by hand, or print with a computer, on the middle of each piece of thin card.
   b. Help your child to glue pictures of good food around the words. You may like to cut these out first, to save time.
   c. When each placemat is finished, cover it with protective adhesive covering film, or take it to be laminated at a print shop.
2. Use these placemats at a family meal during Thanksgiving.
3. The pictures can help remind your child of different things to be thankful for when they say grace before meals.

Another option:

- Write a simple grace on the placemat, and teach it to your child.

Just for you:

- What "graces" do you say before meals? Do you say the same things every time? It's easy to say a quick sentence and not even think about what is being said, or even to feel thankful.

"Give thanks in all circumstances" (1 Thessalonians 5:18).

73

Noah's ark birthday party

Bible story:
Noah's ark—Genesis 6–9

THINGS YOU NEED:

- Noah's ark stationery
- animal face masks for children, or face paints
- party favor bags with items such as tiny Noah's ark storybooks, stickers, and animal-shaped erasers.
- video of the story of Noah's ark
- blue frosted cake with a Noah's ark motif

Worship activities:

1. This party can be a gentle outreach party, because the story of Noah is well known and usually not threatening to non-Christians.

2. Create special invitations for the children you wish to invite.

3. You could hold this party at a zoo! Or you could invite the children to come as different animals, or offer them a mask or a painted face when they arrive.

4. Pray with your child for those coming to the party.

5. Use animal-shaped cutters to cut sandwiches and cookies.

6. Instead of playing games, the children could create animals out of chenille pipe-cleaners, watch the Noah video, or play games about animals.

7. Give out Noah-themed party bags.

8. When everyone has gone, thank God for a happy party.

Another option:

- Perhaps your child could sponsor an animal at a local zoo. God has given people the job of looking after His creation, including caring for the animals.

Just for you:

- What are you and your family doing to help protect the earth? How can you help your child learn to take care of God's creation?

"How many are your works, O Lord! In wisdom you made them all; the earth is full of your creatures" (Psalm 104:24).

Prince or princess for a day!

Bible stories:
The New Jerusalem—Revelation 22
Mephibosheth—2 Samuel 9
King Joash—2 Kings 12
King Josiah—2 Kings 22; 23

THINGS YOU NEED:
- anything to make your child feel like a prince or princess for the day!
- crown
- special clothes
- your child's favorite foods for every meal
- special cloth to cover your child's chair

Worship activities:
1. Help your child feel like a princess (prince for a boy):
    a. Let the child dress up if she likes to.
    b. Serve her favorite foods (whatever they are).
    c. Grant three special requests for the day. (Offer the child five possible choices to limit the requests to things you would be willing to do!)
2. In worship time talk about how this is a special day and your child is being a princess just for today.
3. Tell your child that in God's eyes she is a princess every day, and everybody else is a prince or princess in His eyes also.
4. In heaven everyone will be princes and princesses forever, and they will have a real gold crown and special clothes to wear. In heaven they will have all the time they ever need to do what they want to do. Their choices won't be limited in heaven!
5. Thank God that we are all princes and princesses in His kingdom because He is the King and we are all His children.

Another option:
- Do this on your child's half birthday, or on any day that suits you as a family; it doesn't have to be limited to birthdays.

Just for you:
- What does it mean for you that you are also a prince or princess in God's kingdom? What difference can that thought make to you today as you celebrate with your child?

74

"So you are no longer a slave, but a son; and since you are a son, God has made you also an heir" (Galatians 4:7).

75

You have grown!

Bible story:
Jesus as a child—Luke 2

THINGS YOU NEED:
- photograph albums with pictures of your child since birth
- baby clothes and toys and things the child was given when she was born

Worship activities:
1. Have a cozy time with your child, looking at the pictures of her over the years.
2. Help your child to see how she has changed.
3. How does she look different?
4. How much has she grown?
5. What can she do differently?
6. How do her baby clothes look next to the clothes she is wearing today?
7. What can she do now that she couldn't do a year ago?
8. What special things happened in the last year?
9. How much taller is she than she was at her last birthday?
10. What would your child like to thank God for on her birthday?
11. Thank God for another year of your child's life.

Other options:
- Perhaps you can show video pictures of your child as she has grown up.
- If you use a paper height chart, write on the chart some of your child's special accomplishments through the year, and thank God for them.

Just for you:
- How has your child grown spiritually through the year?
- How have you grown? Sometimes when our children are small, we may feel as though we don't have much time and space to grow spiritually.
- Is there anything you can do to find this space for yourself?

"And the child grew and became strong; he was filled with wisdom, and the grace of God was upon him" (Luke 2:40).

76

Birthday blessings

Bible stories:
Isaac blesses Jacob and Esau—Genesis 27:1-40
Jacob blesses his sons—Genesis 49:1-28

THINGS YOU NEED:

* pen and paper
* optional: candles and perfume or aftershave

Worship activities:

1. Many families give their children a special blessing on their birthdays. This can become a special moment together.

2. Write down a special blessing for your child. To get some ideas, look at some of the biblical blessings and use simple Bible promises.

3. On your child's birthday, as you are putting her to bed, lay your hand gently on the child's head and pray the special blessing you wrote.

4. Keep the written blessings in a special place to reread from year to year.

Another option:

* Place a drop of your favorite perfume or aftershave (depending on the sex of the child) on the child's head as you bless him or her, to add a special fragrance to the moment.

Just for you:

* Being anointed by a friend or spouse can be a special moment. Take a drop of olive or almond or scented massage oil on your finger and anoint the palm of your friend's hand. Bless them in any way that seems appropriate. Especially bless them as parents.

* The priestly blessing below is a good blessing to share.

"'The Lord bless you and keep you;
the Lord make his face to shine upon you and be gracious to you;
the Lord turn his face toward you and give you peace'"
(Numbers 6:24-26).

77

When you are away from your child

Bible stories:
Isaac and Rebekah say Goodbye to Jacob—Genesis 27:41–28:5
Jesus goes back to heaven and leaves His friends—Luke 24:50-53

THINGS YOU NEED:
- attractive box or gift bag
- written or photocopied instructions for a worship activity
- all the materials needed for the worship
- attractive card for your child
- small gift on the theme of the worship
- gift-wrap, adhesive tape, bow, and gift tag

Worship activities:
1. Make a "worship in a box" kit!
   a. Put together everything you need for a worship activity, plus a personal note and a little gift, and place it in an attractive box or gift bag.
   b. Write on the tag when it is to be given to the child.
2. Leave the worship kit with those who are caring for your child.
3. If you will be away a few days, you may want to make several kits.
4. Using this kit may encourage those caring for your child to continue to have creative worships while you are away.
5. Maybe they will want to try some creative worships in their own home when they experience some for themselves.

Another option:
- Tape a short message on a cassette tape for your child to play, so that she can hear you speak the words for the worship and hear you pray for her.

Just for you:
- Take the time to refresh yourself while you are away. Spend time being spiritually nurtured—find a good book to read on the journey or an uplifting tape or CD to play in the car.

> *"'I am going away and I am coming back to you'"*
> *(John 14:28).*

78

Moving house

Bible stories:
Abram and Sarai—Genesis 12; 13
Naomi and Ruth—Ruth 1
Mary and Joseph—Luke 2

THINGS YOU NEED:

* camera
* scrapbook or photo album

Worship activities:

1. Just before you are going to move, talk to your child about how the move will happen.

2. Perhaps your child could help you to make a memory book about your home before you leave:

   a. With your child, go around your home taking photos of each room before everything is packed up.

   b. Develop the photos and paste each photo onto a different page of the scrapbook or photo album. Talk to your child about her special memories of each room. Write some of her memories on the pages around the photos. Add any other photos you have taken that might illustrate some of these memories.

3. Thank God for the special memories.

Another option:

* When you get to your new home, wrap some tiny gifts and hide them all over the home. As your child searches everywhere for the gifts, she will have a happy introduction to her new home. Maybe the gifts could be things for her new bedroom. Then walk through your new home, blessing the activities of each room with a short prayer.

Just for you:

* Moving can be stressful and full of mixed emotions. What are your happiest memories of the home you are leaving? What are your hopes for life in your new home?

> **" 'As for me and my household, we will serve the Lord' "**
> **(Joshua 24:15).**

When your child is ill

Bible stories:
Jesus and the children—Luke 18:15-17
Jesus and the official's son—John 4:43-54
Jesus heals the Syro-Phoenician girl—Mark 7:24-30

THINGS YOU NEED:

- basket
- items that comfort your child, such as favorite soft toys or a soft blanket
- tissues, moist wipes
- favorite drinks
- favorite music, story tapes
- soothing toys

Worship activities:
1. When your child is ill and out of sorts, she may not feel like participating in worship, and you may need to keep worship time very brief.
2. Talk about how Jesus comforted people who were ill and sad. He liked to sit children on His lap and cuddle them and bless them.
3. Ask your child to choose something from the comfort basket, and then use this to comfort your child.
4. Tell your child that Jesus wants to take away all the illness one day. Tell the child how Jesus wants to comfort us when we feel miserable and ill.
5. Keep the comfort basket close to your child so that she can choose other comforts to enjoy when she likes.

Another option:
- If your child has spots with the illness, let her make spotty food to eat, such as a peanut butter open-face sandwich with tiny dots of red cake-decorating gel or sprinkles. God knows about each spot that your child has and wants her to get better soon.

Just for you:
- Do you have any concerns about your own health, or about someone else's health? Read 2 Corinthians 1:3-5. How can you receive comfort from God in your pain and distress? If God sent you a get-well card, what do you think He would write inside?

"He . . . healed those who needed healing" (Luke 9:11).

80

Seasonal changes—God changes us too

Bible stories:
  Zacchaeus—Luke 19:1-10
  Peter—John 21:15-23
  Paul—Acts 9:1-31

THINGS YOU NEED:
- place to walk with evidence of the changing seasons
- bag for collecting interesting things

Worship activities:

  1. Go for a walk with your child. As you walk, talk about the approaching season.

  2. Look around with your child to find different signs that the season is changing. Look at the leaves on the trees, the flowers, the ground, any birds and animals you might see, seeds and nuts, and other seasonal indicators.

  3. Talk about the changes you can see, and how God uses the changes to help things rest and then grow again.

  4. Look out for the lovely things that come with each new season, and help your child to find them.

  5. What changes are you noticing in your child as she grows and masters new skills? Tell the child about the changes you have noticed.

  6. Praise God for the changes in the seasons. Thank Him for helping us to change as well.

Another option:

  - Create a nature basket in your home and place in it the things that you and your child find during each season.

Just for you:

  - Which of the seasons is most like your experience of life at the moment? Which season would you like to experience next? How has God been helping you to change? What other changes are you hoping to experience?

"There is a time for everything, and a season for every activity under heaven" (Ecclesiastes 3:1).

SECTION 5

Favorite Bible Stories

This section presents a handful of familiar Bible stories. They have been given a fresh approach to provide some interactive and multisensory worship experiences. As you experience these worships, they will probably stimulate other ideas that you can adapt and use with different Bible stories.

81

Noah's ark

Bible story:
Genesis 6–9

THINGS YOU NEED:
- improvised clothing for Bible characters
- several old cardboard fruit cartons and large boxes
- lots of toy animals left around the "worship" room
- umbrella
- plastic screw-top jar filled with small lentils

Worship activities:
1. Act out the story of Noah together:
   a. You could dress up in bathrobes to look like Bible characters.
   b. Create an ark out of the boxes, or underneath a table.
   c. Let your child be Noah, and bring him the animals to go in the ark. Put them in different boxes, to keep them from fighting with each other!
   d. Once all the animals are safely inside the ark, you can climb into the ark with your child. Put up an umbrella over the ark if you like.
   e. Let your child shake the screw-top jar of lentils to make a rain sound. Count to forty as the rain "falls," and then wait a while "for the water to go down."
   f. Then come out of the ark, take all the animals out of the "boat," and put them safely back in their "natural" habitats.
2. Praise God for keeping you all safe! Sing a song about rainbows.

Another option:
- Act out the story with more sound effects, such as sawing wood, hammering nails, animal sounds, rain sounds, and the sound of flapping wings for the raven and the dove.

Just for you:
- Noah had to have incredible faith to build an ark on dry ground and believe that God would flood the earth, yet he still did everything God asked him to do. How would you have coped with this if you were Noah, his wife, or his sons and their wives? What would it have been like to be in the ark all those days on the water, with the animals? What would it have been like to step onto dry land again and know you were the only people in the world?

81

• How does this story help you to find perspective in your own life?

"Noah did everything just as God commanded him"
(Genesis 6:22).

Manna—food from heaven

Bible story:
Exodus 16

THINGS YOU NEED:

- your child's favorite popcorn (or use cereal Os)
- tray
- egg cup
- cereal bowl
- table with a cloth or blanket that comes down to the ground or a small play tent

Worship activities:

1. Set up a "tent" and sit inside the tent with your child as you tell the story.

2. Tell your child how God sent the manna to feed the children of Israel in the desert, when there was no other food.

3. Explain how the food had to be collected and eaten fresh each day, but they could collect twice as much on Fridays, when the extra would keep fresh for the Sabbath. Explain how extra food that was kept on the other days soon spoiled and wasn't good to eat.

4. Place the tray outside the tent, and tip all the popcorn or cereal onto the tray.

5. Send your child out to collect popcorn "manna" each day, by filling a small egg cup with popcorn and then pouring it into the cereal bowl.

6. Eat the popcorn together. Then tell your child it's the next day and to collect more food. Do this five times, once for each day of the week.

7. On the sixth time, tell your child to collect two cupfuls of popcorn. Eat one cup together, and then pretend it is the next day and eat the next cupful.

8. Thank God for providing food for you every day!

Another option:

- Collect the "manna" in a clean egg carton that has six spaces, one for each day. On the sixth day collect extra manna in the egg carton lid.

Just for you:

- How does God provide your family with "just enough" for each day? Are you ever tempted to take more than you need?

"My God will meet all your needs" (Philippians 4:19).

83

The battle of Jericho

Bible story:
Joshua 2; 5:13–6:27

THINGS YOU NEED:
- lots of wooden building bricks or cardboard cartons
- a paper blowout, trumpet, or whistle for each person taking part
- coins (treasure)
- a small doll (Rahab)
- a piece of red ribbon or thread
- a sofa for your "camp"

Worship activities:
1. Together with your child build a city of Jericho out of bricks or boxes. Hide the "treasure" in the middle of the city.

2. Tie a red thread around one of the bricks and place the doll next to the thread. The doll represents Rahab.

3. Tell your child that God commanded Joshua to fight an unusual battle.

4. Each day the soldiers and priests walked once around the city, blowing their trumpets but not saying anything.

5. They did this for six days, so name the days as you and your child walk around the city blowing your trumpets. Each time you finish walking around the city, go back to your "camp" and rest.

6. On the seventh day the soldiers and priests walked around the city seven times. Do this with your child. On the seventh time, as the priests blew the trumpets, everyone yelled loudly, and the walls tumbled down. So toot and yell together as you walk around for the seventh time.

7. Knock the walls down as you yell. Rescue Rahab, and then let your child find the treasure. Tell your child that this treasure was especially for God, and let him take the coins to church for the building fund or for a special project for the homeless.

8. Thank God that when we face things that seem difficult, He always knows a way to help us.

Another option:
- You could sing "Joshua Fit the Battle of Jericho" as you act out this story.

Just for you:
- What are the Jericho walls in your life? Are there walls around rela-

83

tionships, or apparently insurmountable difficulties at work?

• What unusual things might God ask you to do to help break those walls down? What treasures might be found if the walls fell down, and relationships were mended?

"I can do everything through him who gives me strength"
(Philippians 4:13).

Preparing for a special baby

A good time to do this worship may be just before a new baby arrives at your home!

Bible stories:

This can be adapted for any of the stories of a new baby, such as the stories about Sarah, Hannah, Ruth, Elizabeth, or Mary.

THINGS YOU NEED:

- collection of items needed for a new baby (for example, baby clothes, bed linen, diapers, baby toys, wipes, lotions)
- washable baby doll (keep hidden at first)
- baby bath full of warm water
- hooded baby towel

Worship activities:

1. Tell your child a Bible story of a new baby coming into a family.

2. Show him all the little things a baby needs, and how small they are. Remind your child that he was once a tiny baby too, and that you were excited about him coming into your home.

3. Perhaps you could tell your child a special story about how you prepared for his arrival, such as how you decorated his room.

4. Then go and pick up the baby doll. Cuddle the doll in a blanket and show it to your child. Explain that the doll isn't a real baby, but that you can practice taking care of it.

5. Help your child to take off the doll's clothes, and then bathe the doll in warm water and dry it with a hooded towel.

6. If a diaper will fit on the doll, show your child how to put on the diaper, and then re-dress the doll together and let your child hug the doll and sing a quiet song to it.

7. Thank God for babies who bring us lots of happiness, even though they are hard work at times!

Another option:

- Show your child pictures of when he was newborn. Talk about the people who came to visit, the parties you had, and the gifts you were given.

Just for you:

- God is as excited about you as you are about a new baby! Even now that

84

you are an adult, He delights in you and longs to be near you.

• He carries your child "close to his heart; he gently leads those that have young" (Isaiah 40:11). How do you respond to such a loving and caring God?

"As a mother comforts her child, so will I comfort you" (Isaiah 66:13).

85

The tale of two houses

Bible story:
Matthew 7:24-27

THINGS YOU NEED:

- two bowls
- some sand
- flat rock or overturned casserole dish
- plastic bricks (avoid using bricks that interlock securely)
- large pitcher or jug of water

Worship activities:

1. Tell your child the story of the wise and foolish builders. As you do so, place a pile of sand in one bowl, and the flat rock in the other bowl.

2. Build two houses with bricks, one on the sand and one on the rock. Try to make the house on the rock quite stable.

3. Then pour water over the house on the sand. The sand should slip away from underneath it, and the house should collapse.

4. Pour water over the house on the rock. Pour gently so that the house stands firm.

5. Explain to your child that the person who built their house on the rock was like someone who listened to God and acted wisely. It was harder work to build a house on the rock, but it lasted much longer.

6. Sometimes it is hard to obey, but it is the wisest thing to do.

7. Pray that God will help your child to be obedient.

8. Perhaps you could sing the song about the wise man who built his house upon a rock.

Other options:

- Before worship, find a piece of acetate (used to make overhead projector transparencies), a permanent transparency pen, and a nonpermanent transparency pen.

- With the permanent pen, draw a house on a rock. With the nonpermanent pen, draw a house on the sand.

- Place this picture in a bowl, and show it to your child as you tell the story. Then when the rain comes, let your child pour water over the acetate.

- The house on the rock will stay, but the house on the sand will wash away.

Just for you:
• Jesus said that those who put His teaching into practice are like the man who built his home on a rock. What safe principles have you chosen to build your home on? How are you living out these choices in your everyday family life?

" 'Everyone who hears these words of mine and puts them into practice is like a wise man who built his house on the rock' " (Matthew 7:24).

86

Jesus helps at a wedding

Bible story:
The wedding at Cana—John 2:1-11

THINGS YOU NEED:
- a wedding photo, yours or someone else's
- several of your best drinking glasses
- pitcher or jug with nontransparent sides
- unfrozen grape juice concentrate
- glass pitcher or jug of water—correct amount for diluting the grape concentrate

Worship activities:
1. Before the worship time, pour the grape juice concentrate into the nontransparent jug, so that your child doesn't know it is there.
2. Tell your child the Bible story.
3. As you tell how the servants helped Jesus by filling the jars with water, help your child to pour water from the clear pitcher into the nontransparent jug.
4. Then pour the grape juice into the special glasses.
5. The people at the wedding could have drunk water if they were thirsty, but Jesus wanted to give them something special.
6. Drink the juice with your child, and thank God for helping us to have fun.

Another option:
- You might like to add a celebration meal to eat with the grape juice. Lay a white cloth and serve your child using the best dishes you have. Sprinkle your child with confetti.

Just for you:
- When we give Jesus something, even something as ordinary as a cup of water, He can transform it into something beautiful and delicious. What part of your life would you like to invite Jesus to transform today?

"Be transformed by the renewing of your mind"
(Romans 12:2).

87

Jesus calms the storm

Bible story:

Jesus calms the storm—Mark 4:35-41; Luke 8:22-25

THINGS YOU NEED:

- small toy boat
- bowl of water
- drinking straws

Worship activities:

1. Tell your child the story of Jesus calming the storm.

2. Illustrate the story by sailing a small toy boat on a bowl of water.

3. Let your child help you make a storm for the boat.

4. You can tip the bowl gently to make waves. Let your child use the straws to blow a wind on the small boat.

5. When Jesus calms the storm, let the bowl rest and ask your child to stop blowing through the straw.

6. Thank God that He has control over the wind and the waves and the big scary things in life. If your child is afraid of something, pray that God will calm his or her fear.

Another option:

- Do this worship activity when your child is having a bath. Then your child can make the waves and blow the boat at the same time. It may be helpful to have a shallow bath in case the waves get high!

Just for you:

- Do you sometimes feel as though you are in a boat on a stormy sea? Do you sometimes feel out of control? Just as Jesus could control the wind and waves, He can take control of the storms you are experiencing in your life.

" 'Even the wind and the waves obey him!' " (Mark 4:41).

88

Jesus and the children

Bible story:

Jesus and the children—Matthew 19:13-15; 21:12-17; Mark 10:13-16; Luke 18:15-17

THINGS YOU NEED:

- scrapbook
- paper
- pictures from magazines
- glue stick
- scissors
- marker pens

Worship activities:

1. Tell the story about Jesus and the children. Jesus welcomed the children and loved them. He listened to them and told them stories. He blessed them.

2. What would it be like if your child met Jesus?

3. Imagine with your child what it would be like if Jesus came to visit your home.

4. Create a scrapbook together about what the day would be like:
    a. What would you do to prepare for His arrival?
    b. How would you decorate the house to welcome Him?
    c. What food would you like to serve Him?
    d. What would you like to ask Him about?
    e. What would you wear?
    f. What would you like to do with Jesus?
    g. What would you like to show Jesus?

5. Write your child's answers and comments in the book. Glue pictures on the pages to illustrate your child's ideas.

6. Pray, thanking God that He is always in our home, even when we can't see Him.

Another option:

- Jesus liked to hug the children and bless them. Find a comfortable chair and hug your child as you tell them Bible stories, pray with them, and bless them.

Just for you:

- If Jesus spent a morning with you, what would you like to ask Him? What

88

answers do you think He might give? Where would you like to meet Him, and what would you like to do together?

" 'Let the little children come to me, and do not hinder them, for the kingdom of God belongs to such as these' " (Luke 18:16).

89

Little things are important

Bible stories:
Zacchaeus—Luke 19:1-10
Parables of the mustard seed and the yeast—Luke 13:18-21

T H I N G S   Y O U   N E E D :

- collection of little things that are very important such as:
  - key
  - button
  - pencil
  - stamp
  - bag

Worship activities:

1. Collect the small items in the bag. Let your child reach into the bag and try to identify any objects without looking at them.

2. Ask your child why the little things could be important.

3. What other small things are really important?

4. Children are very important. Even though they are little, God can still do great things with them. Children can make a difference in the world by being loving and kind.

5. Little things are also important to God. It matters to Him when we lose our teddy bear. He knows where all the lost socks go; He cares when a little tear rolls down our face; He cares when we cut our finger.

6. Thank God that the little things matter to Him. Praise Him for the tiniest details that He has taken care of in the world, and for the tiny little bugs and seeds He makes.

Another option:

- An older child might like to have a matchbox challenge:
  - Give him a small matchbox and let him fill it with as many different tiny items as he can.
  - How many can he fit into the box? Think about a grain of rice, a lentil, a pin, a button, and other small items.

Just for you:

- When do you feel very small? Do you sometimes feel inadequate as a parent? Even the tiny things you do for your child are very important. God can take the gifts you use for Him and use them to move mountains.

89

"Don't let anyone look down on you because you are young, but set an example for the believers in speech, in life, in love, in faith and in purity"
(1 Timothy 4:12).

90

Dorcas cares for the children

Bible story:
Dorcas—Acts 9:32-43

THINGS YOU NEED:

- stiff cardboard
- colored paper
- scissors
- glue stick
- marker pens

Worship activities:

1. Cut some simple people shapes out of the cardboard. Use a pattern from a book, or use a gingerbread cutter to help you.

2. Tell your child the story of Dorcas.

3. Let your child help you cut out paper clothing shapes to dress the cardboard children (or you might like to cut these out before the worship time). Decorate the clothes with marker pens.

4. Thank God for your clothes and the people who have made them and given them to you.

Another option:

- Use your child's dolls and doll clothes. Take all the clothes off the dolls before worship and then dress them all as you tell the story.

Just for you:

- Dorcas used her talents to bring happiness to others who needed her help. What talents do you have that you can share? Even if you are busy, you may have a skill you could share with someone else.

- What skill do you think God wants you to share with someone today?

"There are different kinds of gifts, but the same Spirit. There are different kinds of service, but the same Lord" (1 Corinthians 12:4, 5).

Instant Bible Games

It's a rainy afternoon, and no one knows what to do. Or you're on a long car journey, and everyone is getting out of sorts. You want to play a Bible game together, but you don't have much time to plan anything, and the children are bored with their usual games.

Here are a few instant games to keep in mind. These games have all been designed to be noncompetitive, but you could make them competitive if you wish.

91

Bible sculpties

THINGS YOU NEED:
- modeling clay, Play Doh, or homemade play dough (see recipe below)
- plastic or vinyl cloth to protect the table
- anything that molds dough—cutters, plastic knives, toothpicks, etc.

Worship activities:
1. Let the participants mold their dough into an object from the Bible.
2. When everyone has finished, each person has to try and guess what the object is, and tell which Bible story it comes from.

Other options:
- Set a timer and have everyone make their models within a fixed time.
- If you are traveling, do this activity on plastic plates and use only plastic knives and forks to help with the modeling.

Homemade play dough
- 2 cups all-purpose flower
- 1 cup salt
- 2 cups water
- 2 Tblspns oil
- 2 teaspoons cream of tartar—this is important for helping to preserve the dough
- food coloring (optional)

Add everything to a heavy-bottomed pan. Heat gently and keep mixing well until everything turns gooey. As soon as the mixture starts to come away from the sides of the pan, it's ready. It's important to cook this mixture just right or it will be too runny or too stiff. Knead well, and leave to cool. It will keep for months in a plastic bag in an airtight container.

92

Bible tearaways!

THINGS YOU NEED:

- plain sheets of paper

Worship activities:

1. Give everyone a sheet of paper.

2. Ask them to tear, scrunch, or shape it in any way they like to make something from a Bible story.

3. Let each person show the others what they have made, and see if they can guess what it is and which story it comes from.

4. If this is too hard for your child, suggest something for her to make.

5. Alternatively, your child could suggest an object and you could make it.

Other options:

- Narrow down the possibilities by asking everyone to make something from one specific Bible story.

- Let each person make a paper gift for the person on their right. These gifts can represent something they would like to give the person if they could.

93

Construct-a-story

THINGS YOU NEED:
- construction set of any kind, with interlocking building blocks

Worship activities:

1. Use the building bricks to work with your child to create a scene from a Bible story.

2. Try the Tower of Babel, the battle of Jericho, the Nativity, the paralyzed man being let down through the roof, and other stories.

3. Ask your child about her favorite story and see if you can create the scene together out of the building bricks.

4. Try to use your child's ideas and let her be the architect of the design, but you may need to offer construction tips along the way to minimize frustration if your child has very creative ideas.

Other options:

- Instead of using a construction toy, use everyday things around the home to create much bigger Bible story scenes. For example, turn a table or cupboard into Noah's ark and fill it with animals. Or turn a huge blue sheet into a whale. Include other props from around the home to add extra touches to the scene.
- If lots of people are visiting in your home, form groups and create scenes in your different rooms. Children and adults could act out different characters, and you could have the raising of Jairus's daughter in a bedroom, feeding the five thousand in the dining room, Noah's ark in the bathroom, and a tent scene in the yard! Then do a tour, visiting the different tableaux together.

94

Hide-and-sheep!

THINGS YOU NEED:

- toy sheep
- or cardboard cut-out of a sheep

Worship activities:

1. Tell your child the simple story of the lost sheep.
2. Play hide-and-seek with the sheep toy.
3. Take turns hiding the sheep and letting the other person find it.
4. When the sheep has been found, do some noisy rejoicing!

Other options:

- Let you or your child be the sheep and choose a place to hide.
- Maybe you could wear a woolly sweater or something that looks a bit sheepish.
- Perhaps you could make quiet sheep sounds to help your child find you.
- Don't forget to rejoice when you have been found!
- Or try the lost coin. Hide a large coin for your child to find instead.
- You could hide lots of coins in a room and ask your child to find them and put them in a charity collection box.
- If you have a Noah's ark memory game with matching animal cards, select a few matching pairs. Separate the pairs into two identical piles. Shuffle one set and hide them around the room. Give everyone one of the remaining partner cards. Then let them go and find the animal that matches theirs.

95

Bible scavenger hunt

THINGS YOU NEED:

• paper bags

Worship activities:

1. Give each person a paper bag and a ten-minute time limit. Send them to find as many different things as possible that remind them of Bible stories.

2. When the time is up, call them back and see what they have found.

3. Let them take turns showing what they have found, and let everyone else guess which story it reminded them of.

Other options:

• Send everyone off to look for one thing at a time.
• If it would be hard for your child to think of things on her own, tell her what to search for and see if she can think of the Bible story connection by herself.
• Some ideas:
    • stones—David and Goliath
    • toy animal—Noah's ark
    • cup—the Last Supper
    • bread—feeding the five thousand
    • baby doll—Jesus' birth
    • star—the wise men
    • gold—the wise men
    • perfume—Mary anointing Jesus' feet

96

Fishers of men

THINGS YOU NEED:

- dowel rod or a ruler
- string about twenty-four inches (60 cm) long
- magnet
- pictures of people, glued onto card and cut out
- paper clips
- box
- picture of a church

Worship activities:
1. Tie one end of the string onto the ruler.
2. Tie the magnet into the other end of the string.
3. Clip paper clips onto the cardboard people.
4. Put the people into a box.
5. Fish for the people using the magnetic fishing rod.
6. Place the caught people on the church picture.
7. Explain to your child what Jesus meant when He asked His disciples to be fishers of men.

Other options:
- Use a purchased magnetic fishing game and talk about how Jesus helped His disciples catch fish.
- Or use the purchased game and swap the fish for the cardboard people. You might like to turn the cardboard tank inside out so that the people aren't being fished out of the water!

97

Rainbow search

THINGS YOU NEED:
- pieces of paper in the colors of the rainbow: red, orange, yellow, green, blue, indigo, and violet

Worship activities:
1. Place the pieces of paper on the table in the rainbow color sequence (red, orange, yellow, green, blue, indigo, violet).

2. Ask your child to find objects that are the same colors as the pieces of paper.

3. Start by asking for one object per color, but if this is too easy for your child, then see if she can find three, or even more, per color.

4. Talk about how God has given us the rainbow as a promise to us of His protection.

Other options:
- If you have more than one child, give each a different color to search for.
- This can be done in the house or out in nature. Discourage children from picking whole flowers. They can be careful and take just one petal if you show them how.
- If you are in a car, do this activity by looking for red things outside. When you have found three red things, look for orange things, and so on.

98

Create an animal

THINGS YOU NEED:

- brown paper lunch sack for each person
- assortment of items for each bag:
  - 2 drinking straws
  - 1 piece of kitchen foil
  - 4 plastic forks
  - 1 balloon
  - 1 paper plate
  - 1 paper bowl
  - 4 paper clips
  - 4 sticky stars
  - 1 plastic spoon, etc.
- adhesive tape
- stapler
- scissors
- marker pens

Worship activities:

1. Give each person or group a bag of objects and ask them to create an animal using as many items in their bags as they wish.

2. You might like to pair young children with an adult to help them.

3. When they have finished, they must give the animal a name and say where it would live and what it would eat.

Other options:

- Provide a different set of items and ask each person or group to create a new flower, and say what it is called and where it would be found.
- Use pieces of fruit and vegetables and cocktail sticks to create edible animals.
- If you are on a nature hike, let each person collect a few things along the way to create a creature at the end of the walk.

Creation seek and find

THINGS YOU NEED:

• large dice

Worship activities:

1. One person throws a die. The number on the uppermost face represents one of the days of Creation.

2. That person is sent to find something created on the day they rolled.

3. So a person who rolled a three would go and find a flower, something made of wood, a fruit or vegetable, or a seed, or some other plant item.

4. These items are brought back to show the group, and then the next person rolls the die.

5. This activity helps children learn the days of Creation.

Other options:

• Everyone could roll dice, get a different number, and then go and hunt at the same time.

• Group together all the items that represent a specific day, so that you have all the day three items in one place, all the day four items in another, and so on, and create a display together.

• This game could also be played outside in a forest or park. Keep children safe by pairing them with adults.

Scripture ball game

THINGS YOU NEED:

- Bible
- soft ball

Worship activities:

1. Choose a simple text for your child to learn.

2 The person starting the game recites the whole Bible text and encourages everyone else to say it together. He or she holds the ball and then says the first word in the text again.

3. The ball is then thrown to someone else, and the leader helps that person to say the first word in the verse, and to add on the second word.

4. When the second person can repeat the two words correctly, the second person throws the ball to the next person, and so on, until everyone has memorized the whole verse.

Another option:

- Play this game using Bible names instead. The first person says one Bible name, the second says the first Bible name and adds another, the third says the first two names and adds another one, and so on.

If you enjoyed this book, you'll enjoy these as well:

100 Creative Prayer Ideas for Kids
Karen Holford. Do you or your children struggle to know what to say when asked to pray? Is prayer time becoming routine around your house—even boring? Here are 100 Creative Prayer Ideas that are guaranteed to make time with Jesus interesting, meaningful, and even fun.
0-8163-1968-5. Paperback
US$11.99, Can$17.99.

Making Sabbath Special
Céleste perrino Walker. The art and joy of Sabbath keeping is becoming lost. Here's a book designed to provide simple traditions to make the day a delight.
0-8163-1706-2. Paperback.
US$9.99, Can$14.99.

Family Sabbath Traditions
John and Millie Youngberg. An inspirational and practical guide to help your family fill the Sabbath hours with joy. Two cover options!
Caucasian family: 0-8163-1848-4. Paperback.
African-American family: 0-8163-1854-9. Paperback
US$9.99, Can$14.99 each.

Joyous Christmas Traditions
Evelyn Glass. A nostalgic and fun guide to making the holidays memorable and fun for everyone. Includes favorite holiday recipes, seasonal stories, and more.
0-8163-1797-6. Paperback
US$9.99, Can$14.99.

Order from your ABC by calling **1-800-765-6955**, or get online and shop our virtual store at **www.AdventistBookCenter.com**.
• Read a chapter from your favorite book
• Order online
• Sign up for email notices on new products

Prices subject to change without notice.